Mr. O'Grady,

I hope you enjoy this book!

– Farah

P.S. You will have a quiz over this at the end.

PORTRAIT OF PAKISTAN

PORTRAIT OF PAKISTAN

M. Hanif Raza

FEROZSONS (Pvt.) LTD.
LAHORE KARACHI RAWALPINDI

Photography & Text by M. Hanif Raza

ISBN 969 0 10105 6

First Published in Pakistan 1994 by
Ferozsons (Pvt.) Ltd.
60, Shahrah-e-Quaid-e-Azam Lahore–Pakistan
277, Peshawar Road, Rawalpindi
Mehran Heights, Main Clifton Road, Karachi

M. Hanif Raza

Portrait of Pakistan

Photographs on title cover and on pages 65, 80, 83, 90, 91, 151,
from photo library of Ferozsons (Pvt.) Ltd.

Typeset in 10.5 on 12.5 point Leawood Book
Printed and bound in Pakistan by
Ferozsons (Pvt.) Ltd., Lahore.

Previous page: Islamabad – The nerve-centre of the Country. Offices of various ministries are located in these buildings known as Pakistan Secretariat.

CONTENTS

LAND & PEOPLE 11

HIGHLIGHTS OF HISTORY 57

PAVILIONS OF THE PAST 71

INTERESTING PLACES 97

Overleaf: A fertiliser factory, located near Multan on the Khanewal–Multan road.

PAKISTAN
Provincial Capital
Cities
Km.
100 50 0 100 200
Km.
Miles
50 25 0 50 100
Miles
CHINA
AFGHANISTAN
IRAN
INDIA
ARABIAN SEA
BALUCHISTAN
SIND
PUNJAB
JAMMU & KASHMIR
(DISPUTED TERRITOR)
Karakoram
Great Himalayas
Hindu Kush
GILGIT AGENCY
CHITRAL
Chitral
Tirich Mir 25,260
26,660 ft.
Rakaposhi 25,550 ft.
Hispar Glacer
K2 28,250 ft.)
Baltore Glacier
Siachen Glacier
Gilgit
Nanga Parbat
26,660 ft.
KOHISTAN
Dasu
Dir
DIR
SWAT
Saidu
BAJAUR
MALAKAND
Malakand
MOHMAND
MANSEHRA
Mansehra
MARDAN
Mardan
PESHAWAR
Peshawar
ISLAMABAD
Islamabad
Abbottabad
ABBOTTABAD
KHYBER
Parachinar
KURRAM
ADAMKHEL
Kohat
KOHAT
Attock City
ATTOCK
Rawalpindi
RAWALPINDI
Jhelum
JHELUM
Miram Shah
AHMADZAI
N. WAZIRISTAN
Bannu
BANNU
Mianwali
BHAITTANI
Wana
S. WAZIRISTAN
DERA ISMAIL KHAN
Dera Ismail Khan
Takht-i-Sulaiman 11,100
LARGHA SHIRANI
MIANWALI
Gujrat
GUJRAT
Gujranwala
GUJRANWALA
Sialkot
SIALKOT
SARGODHA
Sargodha
Sheikhupura
SHEIKHUPURA
Lahore
LAHORE
JHANG
Jhang
Faisalabad
FAISALABAD
KASUR
Kasur
MUZAFFARGARH
Muzaffarghar
MULTAN
Multan
SAHIWAL
Sahiwal
VIHARI
Vihari
Bahawalnagar
BAHAWALNAGAR
Dera Ghazi Khan
DERA GHAZI KHAN
Bahawalpur
BAHAWALPUR
Indus
RAHIMYAR KHAN
Rahimyar Khan
Thar Desert
ZHOB
Zhob
PISHIN
Pishin
QUETTA
Quetta
SIBI
Sibi
LORALAI
Loralai
Kohlu
KOHLU
Nushki
KALAT
Kalat
Dadhar
KACHHI
CHAGAI
Kharan
KHARAN
Dera Murad Jamali
NASIRABAD
Jacobabad
JACOBABAD
Khuzdar
KHUZDAR
Panjgur
PANJGUR
TURBAT
Turbat
Gwadar
GWADAR
Uthal
LASBELA
LARKANA
Larkana
Sukkur
SUKKUR
Khairpur
KHAIRPUR
Dadu
DADU
NAWABSHAH
Nawabshah
Sanghar
SANGHAR
Hyderabad
HYDERABAD
Mirpur Khas
THARPARKAR
KARACHI
Karachi
BADIN
Badin
Thatta
THATTA

LAND & PEOPLE

THE LAND

Pakistan was born in 1947. It means the land of the pure – a homeland for the Muslims. Pakistan is one of the important countries of South Asia. It is a young country but the territories it comprises of are as ancient as earth itself. It is a country which offers to its visitors an extremely rich cultural heritage, adventurous regions, magnificent mountains, deserts, verdant valleys, plains and an interesting variety of attractions.

This land has been attracting, from times immemorial, adventurers and invaders, kings and queens, saints and scholars, artists and artisans, traders and travellers, scientists and sportsmen from all walks of life and from all parts of the world.

Throughout the ages it has been the cradle of some of the greatest civilizations the world has known, beginning with the pre-historic Indus Valley Civilization, which had contacts with the other two contemporary and celebrated civilizations of the ancient world, that is, Mesopotamia and Egypt. There are colourful accounts of how this land has appeared throughout the ages to foreign observers from Magasthenese and Marcopolo down to prolix and non too accurate modern chroniclers.

For the present day visitors Pakistan spreads out to a vast landscape of 796,095 sq.km. full of variety and richness. The variety of its attractions is such that almost every visitor can find something to his own liking and choice. For the lovers of adventure and sports there is a different world available in its northern regions where men face the mountains – the Karakorams, the Himalayas and the Hindu-Kush. These are the highest mountains in the world and nature's spectacular work upon earth, mysterious, mighty and majestic.

In fact, the northern region of Pakistan is a marvellous mosaic of small regions, which look similar but not merely standard repetitions. Even a simple topographic description of this multitude of little worlds, Gilgit-Hunza-Sust-Skardu-Shigar-Khaplu–Concordia–would fill a volume of Himalayan dimensions; while structure and genetics are either in excessive detail for smaller areas, or in excessive vagueness for vast areas.

Here, rather than on the Pamirs, is the roof of the world, a mass of rock and ice extending for 250 miles (402 km.) from the Shyok to the Hunza, with the greatest assemblage in the world of giant peaks–Thirty-four over twenty-four thousand feet (7,315 m.) culminating in the tremendous heaps of the three Gasherbrum summits, all over 26,000 ft. (8,000 m.) and finally K-2. The second highest peak of the world. It is an almost regular cone of ice and limestone on a granite/gneiss base, at 28,251 ft. (8,611 m.).

revious pages:
eft: Beaches, five hundred kilometer long and unny throughout the year.

ight: About eighty percent people of Pakistan re agriculturists. Mechanisation in progress.

verleaf: The Batura glacier, as seen from the arakoram highway.

Above: A mountaineering expedition is waitin for the clear weather.

Opposite: The most breathtaking and difficu mountain of the world, which is a passion fo all mountaineers for conquering. This pride c Pakistan is majestic at the height of 28,25 feet (8,611 meters).

Some of the great glaciers of the Karakorams are well-known to mountaineers from various parts of the world who are attracted to this part of Pakistan every year. The most traversed is the Baltoro. Almost all expeditions to the great peaks such as K-2, Broad peak, Hidden peak and Gasherbrums have to walk over this glacier for several days. Some other glaciers also join Baltoro such as Biafo, Chogolisa, Gasherbrum and Godwin Austen, etc. Their confluence is known as Concordia which is considered as a Makkah for all mountaineers because seven of the seventeen highest peaks of the world are located within a radius of twelve miles.

Concordia, the chaotic jumble of ice and rock is far removed from human habitation. It is the wildest wilderness on earth where no human being can survive for long. No doubt man can inhabitate swamps and deserts and even the Polar regions but no living thing can exist in this frozen fastness. Mother nature has added several other features to enhance the beauty of this wonderland including scores of rills, wriggling across the bleak terrain, sprawling and contracting, flooding and freezing with the seasons. Blinding snow storms, piercing wild winds, tumbling temperatures are some of the other features of the region.

The inner sanctum of the Karakorams is accessible only by trails that zigzag along sheer canyon walls, barren except where human hands have transformed them, by irrigation into glistening oasis. There are hundreds of valleys which are isolated even today. Such valleys can only be approached by means of animal caravans or on foot as the trading caravans did through the past centuries. Through these mountains lie precarious links and hazardous trading routes along which merchants and missionaries, travellers and traders struggled in pursuit of trade, education

Opposite: The west wall of the Khunjrab top. It connects Pakistan with China and is one of the highest and difficult passes of the world (16,200 feet).

Below: A common scene from the Kohistan district.

Page 18: When the glaciers melt the water slips out in several forms and shapes. Here is a waterfall several hundred feet high.

Page 19: Road to Kalam, the most popular tourist resort of Swat Valley.

and enlightenment. Their travelling accounts are full of hardships and monsters not seen but much heard of. There are tales of legendary cities of the east visited by them and the stories of silk, gold, jade, diamonds, queens and kings.

There are certain landmarks which are equally grand and awe-inspiring. If K-2 is considered as the pride of the Karakorams then Nangaparbat, about one hundred and fifty miles away from it, is the pride of the Himalayas. It is separated from the main mass by the valleys of Kishen Ganga and Astore between which lies the Burzil Pass; and to the north and east it is moated by the deep gash of the Indus gorges.

Nangaparbat massif carries about one hundred square miles (259 sq. km.) of snow-fields draining into small glaciers descending nearly 8,000 ft. (2,440 m.) below the snowline. Several erosion platforms can be traced, especially notable at just over 13,000 ft. (3,960 m.) where the rounded and flattened ridges and broad rudimentary valleys cut short in front resemble the old morphology of the Deosai plateau. Yet perhaps no mountain in the world is quite so impressive; certainly not Everest, perhaps not even K-2. This is due to the intense erosion around it; the land falls to the north by 23,000 ft. in just fifteen miles (7,041 m. in 22 km.) and the falls to the west-east are nearly of the same order. Vast morains and talus slopes hardly soften a relief which includes precipices of 12,000-13,000 ft. (3,660–3,960 m.) nicked by tiny hanging valleys and glaciers. Round this massif the great Indus flows in gorges 15,000 to 17,000 ft. (4,572 - 5,182 m.) deep and two to four miles wide only. The floor itself is relatively flatish, hot and arid "a desert embedded between icy gravel." Suddenly ahead of it stands the tremendous range of the Hindu Kush and beyond that the windy plateaux of the Pamirs. Northwards the wall of Karakorams continues unbroken. Caught in the grip of three mountain systems the Indus swirls briefly to the north and west but there is no way out there. Hence it must turn south.

Along the banks of the river Indus an eighth wonder of the world has been created by Pakistan and China in the form of a highway known as the Karakoram Highway (K.K.H.). This highway has broken the centuries old isolation of thousands of valleys. Another road is being developed which will connect the Astore valleys complex system with the rest of the country. This road will pass through the Deosai Plateau which is yet another wonder. It is spread over several hundred square miles varying in height from 15,000 ft. to 17,000 ft. (4,572 to 5,182 m.) surrounded by high hills. It is dissected by several streams and there are a few lakes as well. The plateau remains snow bound for more than six months in the year but looks green during summer because long grass covers almost all of its uneven surface. The absence of wood for fuel, the distance from human

Previous Page: Autumn changes the entire landscape of the beautiful Northern areas of Pakistan. Here is Hunza as seen during Autumn.

Opposite: Nagar Valley as seen from Karimabad. The Karakoram highway and the river Hunza separates the Hunza and the Nagar Valleys.

habitations and local superstitions regarding the Devil's *(Deo's)* place prevent people from using the pastures. During the summer some of the herdsmen camp there alongwith the animals.

At the far end of the Deosai lies Skardu which serves as the gateway to several great peaks of the Karakorams including K-2, the Gasherbrums and hundreds of others. Yet another highway is being developed which will join the K.K.H. and that is the Gilgit–Chitral road. This road passes through the heart of the Hindu-Kush which has its own grand pillar–the Trichmir 25,230 ft. (7,690 m.). The main peak is surrounded by several others and some of the grand glaciers. It does indeed look like the mass of frosted silver. Tirichmir has dangerous icefalls. For several centuries the peak was feared. Nobody dared to approach the peak and there were several legends in circulation. It was believed that the peak is defended by giant frogs and locals called them *Boguzai.* The local people also believed that there are fairies in the guise of beautiful girls who meet the climbers with bowls of milk or blood. Those who accept the blood will

Above: Jamia Masjid–Gilgit.

Opposite: A scene from Khaploo Valley.

never see their homes again and those who accept the milk go mad.

From the forbidding heights of the Karakorams, the Himalayas and the Hindu-Kush down to the sea, the 4,000 k.m. long panorama of nature is interspersed with man-made splendours in a fine blend of man and nature at peace with each other yet agreeably individualistic. The central part of the country comprises of plains, deserts and plateaus dissected by several rivers, streams and a complex system of canals as well as dried-up rivers and *nullahs.* Sixty-four percent population of Pakistan lives in the fertile plains of the Punjab. It is the only province which touches all the provinces of Pakistan i.e. Baluchistan, N.W.F.P., Sindh and Azad Kashmir.

Kashmir is bounded by Pakistan–Afghanistan–China and a strip of land not more than thirty miles in the south east of India. This strip of land was awarded to India by the British which upset the National Division announced earlier in June 1947. In the final announcement of August 1947 – the districts of Gurdaspur and Ferozepur, which were undoubtly Muslim majority areas, were awarded to India; all against the mutually agreed to formula as well as against the earlier announcement of June 1947. This was intentionally done in order to provide some route to India so that the Kashmir problem could be kept alive and situation could be exploited by vested interests.

A few miles below the towering heights of the Karakorams, the Himalayas and the Hindu-Kush are several sub-montane regions of great interest including the plains of Peshawar, Kohat and Bannu, all west of the Indus. The Pothwar Plateau is east of the Indus and the salt range, marks the southern boundary both in Bannu and Pothwar. In the past, the Peshawar plains attracted scores of invaders and the Khyber Pass, located at the mouth of the Peshawar Valley, witnessed bloodshed not once but numerous times. The Peshawar valley has probably been the most usual first objective of the invaders. Its tough un-civilized hillmen offered little in the way of taxable capacity and much in the way of administrative strain though strategic roads and key nodal points were firmly held, and formed basis for punitive action, but the tribes governed or misgoverned themselves. So the situation often remained unstable.

On the easternside of the Indus lies Pothwar, spread over an area of 4,000–5,000 square miles (10,360-12,950 sq.km.), average height about 1,200–1,900 ft. (366–580 m.) above sea level. There are a few outlying spurs of the salt range in the south, and Khair-i-Murat Kalachitta mountains in the north are thinly covered with wild, olive bushes and other unproductive wild growth. It is a generally open and undulating area developed mainly around the sandstone Siwaliks and mantled by varying thickness of loessic salt which erodes easily into deep canyons.

Above: Valley Garam Chashma–Chitral. It is well-known for its hot springs and natural beauty.

Overleaf: A view of the Sharda Valley–Azad Kashmir.

Most of the hills and rivers are bordered by belts of intricately dissected ravine lands, locally called as *'Khuddera'*. The streams are generally deep-set owing to rejuvenation, and of little or no use for irrigation.

In the densely populated Pothwar region of the Punjab, a small enclave has been carved out which is called the Federal Territory. Pakistan's capital, Islamabad, is located in this enclave which is covered on the eastern side by rolling green hills and on the other side by Rawalpindi. Near Rawalpindi and Islamabad are several dams including the largest earth filled dam of the world, the Tarbella Dam. The Khanpur–Rawal–Missriot–Tanaza and Simly dams and lakes are all beautiful places.

The canyoned and eroded landscape is suddenly swallowed by the vast fertile plains of the Punjab. It is well connected with all other parts of the country.

Beyond Punjab lies Sindh, known as the gateway to Islam because it was conquered first by the Muslims in the beginning of the eighth century (712 A.D.). It is fertile wherever irrigated by the canal system but total desert where there are no canals. The natural vegetation of thorn scrub merges into thickets of *Babul* (Acacia Arabica) and tamarisk along the inundable riverain

Above: The ancient Jamrud Fort located at the mouth of the Khyber Pass.

Below: Ducks enjoying the early morning sun.

Overleaf: A bird's eyeview of the Sports Complex in Islamabad.

Opposite: A view of the historic Khyber Pass which is the easiest link between Pakistan and Afghanistan.

tracts. For the next six centuries, whether the entire region was governed by a single powerful emperor or it was divided into a number of independent principalities, it formed part of the world of Islam that extended from Sindh to Spain.

Major part of the province is irrigated by a grand canal system. Seven great canals flow out from the Sukkhar Barrage alone in various directions and irrigate the parched plains spread over thousands of acres. There are several lakes, the largest one is the Manchar which accummulates most of the flood waters of the Indus but drains out again in the Indus when the flood condition recedes.

Above: Pakistan is not rich in forests but the are attractive wherever they are.

Opposite: Tile decoration–Tomb at Hala.

Overleaf: A view of Islamabad, the Capital the Country.

Previous Page: The Rawal lake–Islamabad

Sindh is the birthplace of the world's oldest archaeological sites and civilizations. Moenjodaro, one of the capital cities of the Indus Valley civilization was the first of the great civilizations of the subcontinent. At its height, it encompassed 400 cities and towns extending along the Indus and its tributaries, covering most of the present day Pakistan. Few of the cities of this civilization have been excavated and what little we know of this civilization comes from the excavations of Moenjodaro, near Sukkhar, Sindh, and from Harappa near Sahiwal, Punjab.

In the far south, Baluchistan the largest province of Pakistan is located. It covers a huge area of wild, rugged and sparsely populated country bordering Afghanistan and Iran. It is a arid region enclosed by Tabakakar mountain range along the Afghan border, and by the Suleman range. To the south there is one of the most inhospitable deserts of the world, the Makran.

Further in the South, along the coast from Makran to Karachi, the golden beaches are wide and dotted with mangrove swamps and lagoons.

THE PEOPLE

The modes of living and working of the people of Pakistan were shaped by the geography of the country. Vast plains of fertile land watered by a rivers system provided ideal conditions for agriculture. Large semi-arid regions and well grassed mountain slopes are good for goat, sheep and cattle breeding and the mild climate of the plains provides good chances for trade and commerce.

Pakistan has been the cradle of the world's most ancient civilizations yet it was the conquest of Sindh in 712 A.D. by the Muslims which spread Islam as the main cultural force. Three centuries later its influence was extended from south to north and east to west. With the passage of time Islam became a binding force uniting the multitude of ethnic groups varying in descent, history and way of life. It would be of no purpose to enumerate the names of various tribes of people who live in Pakistan. It would be sufficient to add that more than ninety percent of the people of Pakistan are Muslims. They believe in One God, one Prophet (pbuh) and one holy book *'Al-Quran'.* Minority groups including Hindus, Christians and Parsies constitute about ten percent of the entire population.

Pakistan is divided into four main provinces – Baluchistan, Sind, Punjab and the North-West Frontier Province (NWFP). The Northern Areas and Azad Kashmir are under special administration of the Government of Pakistan because of their strategic location. Punjabi, Sindhi, Pashto and Baluchi are the major languages in use. In addition to these numerous dialects are attached to particular tribes or groups. Urdu is the national language.

Opposite: Dehli Gate of Multan, the ancie living city of Pakistan.

Previous Pages: Tomb of Mir Massoom Shal Sukkur.

Detail in Stone–Tomb Jam Nizamuddi Thatta.

SAHID

Overleaf: Taxila–cultural centre of the Ghandhara empire is now in ruins but tradition continues. An artisan from Taxila is giving final touches to a colourful Jar.

Left: A cattle and goat sale and purchase market.

Right: A master singer musician from Baluchistan.

Below: Tractor driven carts are gradually replacing the centuries old camel driven ones, which have been the most common mode of transportation in the sandy desert of Choolistan.

CENTRE
E M E

ft: A master of one of the army bands in
; typical uniform.

ght top: A smiling farmer from the
njab.

ght bottom: A female singer from Sindh.

'lowing pages: One of the traditional
tures of marriage, 'Mehndi'.

ypical phulkari (shawl). It is one of the
ost popular shawls of Sindh.

Previous pages: One of the busy bazaars of Lahore.

A view of the Sunday Bazaar–Islamabad.

Below: An Eid Mella–Clifton, the popular beach of Karachi.

Opposite top: Clean water – Women have to travel a lot in the Choolistan desert in order to fetch potable water from distant places.

Opposite bottom: A singer from Sindh.

Below: A view of Juma Bazaar–Islamabad.

Today Pakistan is the land of 120 million people, working together for a common objective which appears to be the glory of Pakistan. Their everyday behaviour and expression may appear casual in relation to the various aspects in life, but they are serious workers and their skill and craftsmanship could be compared with the people of the developed world. Their houses in almost all parts of the country still maintain the character of a home, not just a roof and a shelter for a human gathering. Pakistan their home, varies from place to place, expressing the sensitivity and aesthetic culture which is multi-coloured and alive.

HIGHLIGHTS OF HISTORY

ICE AGE

The stone implements recovered from the terraces cut by the river Soan in the material deposited by the melting ice-fields during interglacial phases indicate that the drama of human survival was once staged in Pothwar Plateau around Islamabad, the capital of Pakistan as far back as half a million years ago.

4000–100 B.C.

The materials excavated from Meharghar, indicate that Neolithic agriculturists made their first appearance in the low hilly areas of Baluchistan, the largest province of Pakistan.

At the dim dawn of history this region saw the flowering of the Indus valley Civilization. Improved techniques permitted storage of wheat and barley beyond daily needs and cities grew up at Harappa and Moenjodaro around 2300 B.C. The cities of the Indus Valley Civilization had an efficient underground sewage system.

During the 15th century B.C. the Aryans, as the Hindus label their forefathers, arrived on the scene. They migrated from Central Asia to Mesopotamia and then through northern Iran and Hindu-Kush into the area now known as Pakistan. The Aryans were fair skinned cattle breeders to whom the cow was sacred. The Aryans settled in the Punjab, the land of the five rivers after defeating the local inhabitants. As the land was fertile and water available in plenty, they took to agriculture.

The region of the Punjab was invaded by Takkas. They were Turanians by race and decendants of Zohak, the Iranian king who had a growth of two snake like tumours on his shoulders. The Takkas were snake worshippers. The city of Taxila was founded by them.

Darius Hystaspes, the king of Persia invaded Punjab and annexed this region to his empire, including Taxila.

Xerxes (Kashayarsha) the King of Persia, dominated the north-west region until the end of Achaemenid dynasty.

Alexander the Greek conqueror, overran Iran in 326 B.C., crossed the Indus and marched upon Taxila. Raja Ambhi, the king of Taxila, accepted defeat and he provided an army contingent to Alexander to invade the Punjab. Raja Porus was defeated in the battle fought at Jhelum (Hydaspes). Philip, son of Machatas, was appointed *satrap* of Taxila. He was, however, assassinated and Eudamus was appointed in his place as a temporary measure. Alexander died in 323 B.C. at Babylon.

After the death of Alexander, Chandragupta led a successful revolt against the foreign invaders and Eudamus withdrew from the north-west. Chandragupta became Master of the Punjab and

pposite: Lacework in stone–A close view of e Chowkundi graves.

declared himself as the Maharaja. He also laid the foundations of a strong Maurayan empire.

The Maurayans remained supreme for about a century. In 262 B.C. Ashoka (Mauraya) adopted Buddhism as the state religion. The new faith did not prosper much in *Bharat,* but it flourished in the region now known as the North-West Frontier Province of Pakistan.

Euthydemus took over possession of Paropamisadae, Arachosia and Sistan. In 183 B.C. Demetrius succeeded his father Euthydemus and invaded Gandhara, the Punjab and the Indus Valley. He made Taxila his capital. These Bactrian Greeks ruled over this region for about a century but failed before the onslaught of the Sakas. After the rule of the Sakas or the Parthians came the Kushans.

100–900 A.D.

The Kushans took over charge of this region around 78 A.D. The Kushan period was a period of great activity. It saw the flowering of Gandhara Art. It also saw the expansion of the empire over Kashmir, Kasghar, Khotan, Kabul and a considerable part of India.

The rise of the Sassanian power in Iran and Gupta power in India brought about the weakening of the Kushans. They, however, continued to rule over the north-west areas (of present Pakistan) for another century till the white Huns invaded.

*)pposite: Tomb of Shah Rukn-e-Alam–
Aultan.*

*Below: Archaeological Museum, Taxila–The
'easure trove of the Ghandhara art.*

bove: Moenjodaro (Mound of the Dead) uins.

ˀpposite left: Brahamani Bull–Moenjodaro.

ˀpposite right: King Priest–Moenjodaro.

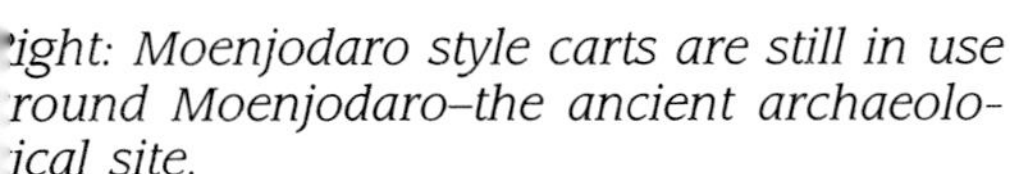

ight: Moenjodaro style carts are still in use round Moenjodaro–the ancient archaeolo- ical site.

Above: Katas–The sacred shrine of the Hindu community–around Choa Saidan Shah.

Opposite: Shahjahan Mosque, Thatta, built during the reign of Emperor Shahjahan.

The Huns Invasion swept over Gandhara and the Punjab. They carried fire and sword wherever they went and spread destruction. They destroyed the Buddhist monasteries and stupas at Taxila and other places.

From Huns sprang Rajputs. Rajput principalities were set up in this region and elsewhere. When *Hieun Tasang,* the Chinese traveller, who came to this part of the country in the 7th century, the ancient glory of Taxila and Gandhara region was over; Buddhism was on the decline. At that time this region was a principality of Kashmir. In the ninth century, around 850 A.D., this region was ruled by the *Turki Shahis* of Kabul who traced their origin from Kanishka.

Along the Sindh-Baluchistan coast, several ships were looted by the Indian pirates. In 711 A.D. these pirates plundered several Arab ships off the coast of Sindh. The Arab Muslims decided to retaliate against the pirates who were supported by the Raja of Sindh, Raja Dahir and sent an army expedition under the leadership of Mohammad bin Qasim. His contingent landed at Debal, a small seaport somewhere around present Karachi. He defeated Raja Dahir who was a strong supporter of the pirates. Sindh was captured. Part of Punjab upto Multan was also captured (712 A.D.).

For nearly 300 years Muslim conquest in India was confined to Sindh and areas upto Multan.

900–1900 A.D.

Towards the end of the 10th century Kabul Valley was won by Islamic forces. In 1008 A.D. Mahmood of Ghazni crossed the Indus and fought fierce battles through the Punjab and Gujrat to the western end of the Ganga valley at Mathura and Kanhauj.

He raided India seventeen times, more to finance his empire in Persia and Turkistan than to establish any permanent foot hold in India. He used the booty collected in these raids to build a library, a museum and a grand mosque at Ghazni. The area upto Lahore was included in his empire.

By the end of the 12th century the Turks commanded by Sultan Mohammad of Ghor and his *Mamlok* (slave) general, Qutab-ud-Din Aibak, seized Ghazni in 1173 and invaded India with Afghan forces. The Hindu Rajas tried their best to face the Muslim forces but failed and were defeated.

By 1193 the Turks became the Masters in Peshawar - Lahore and Delhi. After the death of Sultan Mohammad Ghori, Qutab-ud-Din Aibak became the emperor and consolidated the Sultanate rule in the subcontinent with its centre at Delhi. In 1210 A.D. the *Qutab Minar* at Delhi and the famous mosque *Quwat-al-Islam* were constructed. He lies buried in Lahore in a very simple tomb as he died here while playing Polo.

Changiz Khan, the Mongol, invaded the subcontinent in 1221 A.D. Punjab was captured, sacked and looted. Emperors of the Sultanate period, including Altamish and Ghias-ud-Din Balbun, tried to control the Mongol invasions, but in vain.

The Khilji dynasty took over the government from the Sultanate dynasty during 1290 and Jalal-ud-Din Khilji was the first emperor of this dynasty. Alla-ud-Din Khilji (1296-1315 A.D.) was the best known emperor of this dynasty who enlarged his empire considerably. The successors of Alla-ud-Din Khilji however proved themselves as useless and the kingdom was captured by the Tughlaqs.

Ghias-ud-Din Tughlaq took over as emperor in 1320 A.D. He was succeeded by Mohammad Tughlaq (1325-1351 A.D.) and Firoz Tughlaq (1358–1358 A.D.) *Ibn-e-Batuta,* the famous traveller, visited the subcontinent during 1354 A.D. Tughlaqs constructed some of the most beautiful tombs at Multan. The Tomb of *Shah Rukn-i-Alam* is a masterpiece of their architectural style.

Tamerlane or Taimur the Lame, yet another Mongol conqueror, with his capital at Samarkand invaded the subcontinent in 1398 A.D. He captured the area upto Delhi. The government at the centre fell apart and many small independent states came into being.

The Syed dynasty took over control of the country in 1421

Opposite: Decorated details of Wazir Kha mosque–Lahore.

Above: A partial view of the famous histor[…] Fort–Lahore (Rebuilt and enlarged durin[…] 1566–1674 A.D.).

A.D. and remained in power for about thirty-seven years. This dynasty was succeeded by the Lodhi dynasty and they governed for about seventy-five years.

The Mongols appeared on the scene again in 1526 A.D. and this time under the banner of Babur, a descendant of Changiz Khan and Taimur-Lame. Babur captured the subcontinent and laid the foundation of a great Mughal empire from 1526 to 1805 A.D. Emperors of this dynasty were–Babur, 1526–1530; Humayun 1530-1539; Akbar 1556-1605; Jehangir 1605–1627; Shahjahan 1627–1657 and Aurangzeb 1661–1707. All the successors of Aurangzeb, however, proved themselves as weak and the large empire thus disintegrated.

By the middle of the 18th century the Afghans attacked the Punjab again and again and looted the entire population at will. Ahmed Shah Abdali invaded seven times and sold the Punjab to the Sikhs who crushed the Muslim population. Afghan attacks, however, continued after the death of Ahmed Shah Abdali and Lahore, as well as its surrounding area, was finally sold by the Afghan invader Shah Zaman, the grandson of Ahmed Shah Abdali, to Ranjeet Singh. Ranjeet Singh established a strong Sikh rule in the Punjab and some of the areas even beyond Peshawar.

The Sikh rule, however, did not last long and in a fierce battle with the British the Sikhs were defeated. The Sikh army laid down their arms in 1849 at Rawalpindi. So the Punjab also came under the British rule.

1900–1947 A.D.

Several movements were launched time and again to overthrow the British rule including the War of Independence in 1857 but in vain. In 1930 the poet-philosopher, *Dr. Muhammad Iqbal,* proposed a separate homeland in the north-west of India. A small group of Muslim students at Cambridge led by *Ch. Rehmat Ali* came up with the name of Pakistan, taking the initials of Punjab, Afghani (N.W.F.P.), Kashmir, Sindh and Baluchistan. The Muslim League was formed and the Muslim Leaders' campaign for partition was led very successfully by *Quaid-e-Azam Muhammad Ali Jinnah.* The Pakistan Resolution was formally passed at a mammoth gathering at Minto Park, (now called as Iqbal Park) in Lahore, on March 23, 1940. Pakistan was achieved after several years of efforts and great sacrifices of the Muslim population of the subcontinent.

With the creation of Pakistan on August 14, 1947 the British rule came to an end in the subcontinent. The Pakistan flag was hoisted at a simple ceremony at Karachi which was declared as the capital of Pakistan while Rawalpindi was declared as the General Headquarter of the Pakistan Army.

During 1959 the capital was shifted to the newly selected site of' Islamabad. Keeping in view the fact that development of the new city will take sometime Rawalpindi was declared as the interim capital of Pakistan.

Left: A scene from the Akbar-Nama. Here Bullocks have been shown dragging the siege guns during Akbar's attack on the fort at Ranthambhor. The eyes are led straight to Akbar, at the top of the struggling column, aloof and slightly larger than his companions.

Overleaf: The tomb of Emperor Jahangir, Lahore, built during 1627–1637 A.D.

PAVILIONS OF THE PAST

POTHWAR

If the calculations of the modern science are correct, then implements discovered from the Soan Valley are as old as 500,000 years.

From different accounts Pothwar seems to be the abode of pre-human ancestors, who were the first tool making animals who ever walked on earth. It may, however, be assumed that the ancient people of Pakistan who lived in the Pothwar plateau centuries ago made stone choppers and hand axes. They lived along the banks of the rivers and they were not fully aware of cultivation or flock raising. They lived on fishing, hunting and food gathering from plants and trees. The story of the development of mankind in Pakistan, however, does not end here. It begins, in fact, from here.

MEHERGHAR

Some of the latest excavations carried out in Baluchistan particularly at Meharghar brings to light the facts that about eight thousand years ago, man had already established, though in rudimentary form, village life. These excavations also indicate that man had already learned the art of farming and flock raising. He was living in villages set in the small valleys amongst the hills or occasionally on the great river-plain itself. He had cattle, sheep and goats and horses. He grew barley and other crops and earned an adequate living for himself and his family. His interests were restricted mainly to his own immediate surroundings and limited his contacts with his neighbours. Excavation around Amri, Zhob, and Meharghar indicate that a small village culture flourished between 7000 to 4000 B.C. The people enjoyed a fairly uniform standard of equipment and living. The pottery excavated from these sites, domestic as well as funerary, however, differed considerably in skill and character from place to place. It is, in fact, the pottery which indicate their occasional movement and inter-relationship. According to the studies of various research groups, it may be said that by the beginning of 4000 B.C. the fore-mentioned village groups were perhaps still living in the stone age. They had not yet acquired sufficient knowledge of utile metals such as copper and tin to use them for the manufacture of tools and weapons. By the end of 3000 B.C. both copper and tin were known and their alloy, bronze, was sometimes used.

The excavations of Kot Diji provide important clues to yet another culture which flourished between 3000 to 2500 B.C. Which seems to have influenced various aspects of life and culture of the Indus people.

pposite: Nao-Lakha Pavilion–(Pavilion of ine hundred thousand diamonds)–Lahore. he Pavilion was plundered and diamonds lucked away during the Sikh rule.

INDUS VALLEY

The excavations of Harappa and Moenjodaro suggest that a highly developed civilization lived there about 2500 B.C. That civilization not only possessed a high standard of art and craft but also had a well developed system of pictographic writing. The Indus Valley civilization flourished for a considerable period till the arrival of the Aryan invaders.

The excavations at Harappa, Moenjodaro and other similar sites have provided very useful information about the civilization of the original inhabitants of the subcontinent. The Indus valley civilization can be described as belonging to the Bronze Age because at its prime, wherever excavations have been carried out on wider scale, copper and bronze objects have been found in addition to the stone implements. Absence of iron implements helped the archaeologists to determine this age. Detailed studies of Harappa and Moenjodaro excavations indicate that Indus Valley civilization was contemporary to the early Dynostic Sumerion Civilization. The close resemblance between some of the objects unearthed in south Mesopotamia and the Indus valley lead to that conclusion. Discovery of the seals of Harappa-Moenjodaro origin, containing carvings of the Indus valley animals such as elephants, rhinoceros and buffaloes, from the Mesopotamian sites of Tell Asmar Kish and Ur, is enough to prove this fact.

These excavations also reveal that the economy of the cities of Harappa and Moenjodaro were based on the fertile valleys of the major rivers of the Indus basin which also offered easy means of communication and transportation. Having such advantages at their disposal it was possible for the inhabitants to exchange crop surplus which enabled them to import necessary raw materials such as metals, semi-precious stones and other such commodities from the neighbouring countries. These excavations also provide ample evidence that the people of these cities cultivated wheat, barley, sesame, dates and cotton. The existence of a large number of brick lined street drains and rain water pipes, the use of brunt bricks instead of sun-dried bricks in the buildings and carvings on the seals of such animals as the tiger, rhinoceros, elephants and buffaloes which favour moist habitat, indicates that the Indus valley enjoyed a much heavier rainfall in the ancient times than at present.

The architecture of the Harappa Moenjodaro period is plain and utilitarian rather than ornamental. There are no imposing temples as in Sumer, nor royal tombs as at Ur and in Egypt. It seems that the aim of the city builders was to make life comfortable rather than luxurious. The houses are well planned. There are bathrooms with circular brick lined wells and smooth paved floor sloping off to the bricked-in drain which leads to large covered drains flowing down every street.

Above: A flower vase from Multan.

ɔove: Belle from Bahawalpur area–
ıoolistan.

Various objects of art have been found in these ancient cities. There is a large number of burnt clay male and female figurines and models of animals and birds. The female figurines wear short skirts round their loins, and are profusely bedecked with jewellery and pannier-like arrangement on each side of the ear; some of the panniers are smoke stained, and it is possible that oil, or perhaps incense was burnt in them. These figurines are taken to represent the *'Great Mother goddess'* whose cult was

Above: Bahawalpur Pottery–as light as pape

also widespread in the near Middle-East in ancient times. The male figurines are mostly bearded, and they wear long hair at the back. What diety they represent is difficult to say. It appears that both the male and female figurines were modelled by hand and painted light red.

The figural art however, is best illustrated by steatite seals bearing life-like representations of such animals as the Brahmani Bull, the short-horned bull, buffalo, tiger, rhinoceros, and crocodile, etc. Figures of mythological creatures like the 'unicorn', a human figure with horns and a tail, and a horned tiger have also been carved with perfection. The seals also bear short inscriptions in pictographic script, which have not been decyphered yet.

The commonest ornaments consisted of necklaces and pendants of beads of semi-precious stones. Gold necklaces, fillets for head wear, armlets, bangles and finger rings were worn by both sexes; girdles of long carnelian beads, ear-rings and anklets were exclusively for women.

Copper and bronze were used for making domestic utensils, implements, statuettes and ornaments. The utensils are in the form of pottery vessels and consist of cooking pots, flat dishes, vases and dishes with covers. The tools and implements are common.

The Harappan pottery shows a highly developed technique as is evident from the varied shapes, some of which are comparable with the pottery of the neighbouring countries of Iran and Turkey. The principal forms include offering-stands, pointed bottom goblets, tall beakers, wide/shouldered vessels, narrow-necked vases, dishes, basins, pans, jar-covers, handled cups, feeding cups, perforated heaters and storage jars.

Nobody is sure about the people who lived in Harappa and Moenjodaro. It is certain though that they were of non-Aryan racial stock. They were highly civilized, and not only do their well-built cities bear witness to this fact, but confirmation is also found in various aspects of their religion.

The excavated sites do not provide any clue as to how this

Opposite: The town of Uch is known for beautiful and decaying tombs.

Overleaf: Ancient Chowkundi tombs aroun Karachi.

Above: Dharmarajika Stupa–Taxila.

advanced civilization vanished. It is, however, presumed that progressive desiccation of the Indus valley may have been one of the causes of the decay and desertion of the Harappa culture cities after 1800 B.C. The growing danger of floods may also have been responsible for the evacuation of cities like Harappa and Moenjodaro as both are situated on river banks. The former is on the Ravi bank, and the latter on the right bank of the Indus.

GANDHARA

By 1500 B.C. the Indus valley civilization had vanished. It was not followed by any other important civilization for about one thousand years. However, the excavated remains at Taxila and a number of monasteries and stupas in the north west now bring us down to that period of recorded history. It was no longer an isolated culture. Taxila, though separated by the lofty Hindu-Kush and Himalayas from the neighbouring cities of central Asia, was beyond any doubt, a part of one and the same Buddhist civilization which has been described by the famous Chinese traveller, *Hiuen Tsang* in the following words:

"The kingdom of Gandhara extends about 1000 li from east to west, and about 800 li from north to south. On the east it borders on the river Sin (Sindh-Indus). The capital of the country is called Pol-lu-shapu-lo- (Purushapura-Peshawar). The towns and villages are deserted, and there are but a few inhabitants. At one corner of the royal residence there are about one thousand families. The country is rich in cereals, the climate is warm and moist, and in general without any ice or snow. The nature of the people is timid and soft: they love literature; most of them belong to heretical schools; a few believe in the true law."

It may be noted that Hiuen Tsang's report is dated in the early 7th century A.D. when the peak of Gandhara culture had already passed.

This great empire of Gandhara however fell apart when Alexander invaded that region in 326 B.C. He captured Charsadda (ancient name *Pushkalavati)* located about twenty miles from Peshawar (ancient name *Purasapura)* and then moved eastwards, crossed the river Indus around Hund and forced his way into the Punjab.

A great deal of Gandhara sculptures however survived, dating from 1st to probably as late as seventh century. They had a remarkably homogeneous style. When Peshawar became the winter capital of the Kushan empire in 2nd century A.D. and superseded Charsada as the paramount city of Gandhara, the Khyber became a major Gateway. Traders with luxury goods from China, Central Asia, Persia and Rome jostled through the narrow streets of this great entrepot on the silk route as they still do today.

In their wake came Buddhist missionaries and pilgrims in response to the intense religious revival occasioned by Kanishka's patronage. Several Buddhist monasteries nestled within the folds of the Khyber Pass offered haven. Even the ruins of the Khyber's Sphola stupa proclaim the glory of its day.

Buddhism was revived in the 3rd century A.D. under the dynamic leadership of Ashoka as the old religion was still popular and its promotion appealed to the people at large. Scores of teams of the teachers from Gandhara carried their faith to the Chinese Turkistan and thence to China and to several other countries. Stupas and monasteries were established in various parts of the country. Swat alone claimed more than seven hundred monasteries. The largest and the wealthiest was at *Butkara,* which in the local language means 'Idol temple'. It is located just about a mile from the Swat Museum. The main stupa was ringed by 250 well decorated stupas, chapels and columns. Only small vestiges of the decorations remain on site but choicest samples can be seen even today in the Swat Museum at Saidu Sharif. Scores of fine exhibits and some unique pieces can also be seen in the Dir Museum at Chakdara.

It is believed that the entire area from Peshawar to Gabral and the entire Dir valley were stupa-studded. There were hundreds of monasteries throughout these valleys. Ruins of such monasteries can be seen around Mardan, Jamalgarhi,

Above: Decorated details of Wazir Kh
mosque–Lahore.

Above left: A typical tile pattern from Mult

Shahbazgarhi, Charsadda, Takht-i-Bahi and several other places. The most impressive monastery complex can be seen on the top of a hill known as *Takht-i-Bahi* about eight miles north west of Mardan. Massive walls surround the main sanctuary dating back from the 1st to the 7th centuries A.D. Against the hillside, towards the South, the principal stupa is located in the centre of its own courtyard lined with chapels on three sides, each of which once contained sculptures of *Lord Buddha*. From this courtyard steps lead down to an oblong courtyard filled with the remains of votive stupas and chapels. Some three miles to the south west of *Takht-i-Bahi* there is a village known as *Sahr-e-Bahlol* from the environs of which great quantities of Buddhist sculptures have been recovered during the past hundred years by the smugglers as well as by the archaeologists.

The most important site of the Gandhara period undoubtedly is Taxila which played a great role in the promotion of Buddhism not in this region only but In several other parts of the world also. It was considered as one of the greatest Universities of Buddhism and it was from here that monks and missionaries went to foreign lands through the treacherous mountain ranges. Even today Taxila ruins attracts tens of thousands visitors each year from several parts of the world.

There is, however, no doubt that the story of Taxila began centuries ago when the world was young. Its original name was *Takshasila,* meaning the city of cut stones. This name was later shortened by the Greeks and it was better known to the world as Taxila, the seat of a great oriental culture and learning.

Set in the heart of a picturesque valley, about 20 miles north of Rawalpindi on the Grand Trunk Road, these extinct cities of

ove: Ancient sacred stone carvings–
cred Rock–Hunza Valley.

'Gandhara' survive as witness to the rise and fall of many empires and many civilizations. The sites are surrounded by long stretched green fields dotted by small peaceful villages. Life is as leisurely as reflection itself. Tall verdant trees, with leafy branches nodding in the breeze, seem to whisper of the ages past.

Taxila was a satrapy of the great Achaemenian empire of Persia in the 6th century B.C. and later successively came under the sway of Greek, Mauryan, Bactrian-Greek, Scythian, Parthian and finally the great Kushan Kings. Then came the end of this glorious empire around 455 A.D; with the savage onslaught of the white Huns. The Huns rose from the Central Asia like a thunderstorm and spread terror and destruction as they sped from one country to another, leaving a trail of blood-bath, woes and miseries behind. They stormed the north-western part of the subcontinent and swept off whatever traces of civilization and culture they encountered one their way.

Taxila is world famous for its unique Gandhara Sculptures excavated from Sirkap and from other stupas and monasteries. These exquisite pieces of Gandhara Sculpture have classical Indo-Greek characteristics. The folds of the drapery in stone, the dreamy smiles, the chaste feature derive their inspiration from the Hellenistic School. All pieces show a craftsmanship lost to us today. Most of the antiquities recovered from all these excavations have been displayed in the Taxila Museum. It also has a large and important collection of coins belonging to different periods. There are several other sites where pavilions of the past can be seen. Monastries and remains of the ancient cities are spread over several thousand square miles. Such monasteries and stupas can be seen in Mardan, Takhat-i-Bahi, around Peshawar, in Swat and Dhir Districts. Rocks containing the images of stupas, deities and several other figures can be traced in the districts of Kohistan, Chilas, Hunza and even in Skardu. Lord Buddha cut in stone or carved on huge rocks can be seen in the northern areas also, particularly in Swat, around Gilgit and Skardu.

MUSLIM PERIOD

The people of the South Asia saw the flowering of a new culture and civilization during the early eighth century as Islam was introduced in this region in 711-12 A.D. when *Muhammad bin Qasim* conquered the lower Indus valley and the area upto Multan.

Sindh and Multan attracted Arab travellers, writers and missionaries. They spread their activities into the Punjab, Baluchistan and the tribes of the mountains in the north-west.

The Muslim empire in Sindh continued to exist until the decline of the Umayyads. This conquest also opened the way for new cultural contacts between the Hindus and Muslims.

In the beginning of the eleventh century *Sultan Mahmood of Ghaznavi* annexed Peshawar and the Punjab. Sultan Mahmood invaded India seventeen times. He paved the way for the future Muslim conquests.

The Ghaznavid rule over the Peshawar region, the Punjab and Multan, roughly corresponding to what now constitutes Pakistan, lasted for about two hundred years. It was during this period that Muslim culture in the northern and western areas of Pakistan took roots. After the fall of Ghazni many poets, writers and philosophers, displaced from their homes, settled in Lahore. Lahore which remained the capital of this area till the time of *Altumish.* Persian became the language of culture of the Muslim elite. Lahore played the role of a smaller Ghazni. Three eminent persons are associated with the Ghaznavid Lahore. They are the poet *Mas'ud Sa'd Salman* who wrote in Arabic, Persian and Hindi; the famous *'Ali Hujweri',* known as *'Data Ganj Bakhsh',* the author of *Kashf-ul-Mahjub,* one of the earliest works on sufism; and the famous slave of Mahmood Ghaznavi, *Ayaz. Ali Hujweri* lies buried in Lahore and even today his tomb attracts thousands of people every day from all parts of Pakistan. *Ayaz* is also buried in Lahore where he served as the Governor and built the Lahore Fort which was enlarged and almost rebuilt by Akbar, the great Mughal king.

No doubt Mahmood Ghaznavi succeeded in shattering the power of the Hindus but he failed to establish a strong Muslim empire in the subcontinent. It was *Muhammad Ghori* who took advantage of the situation and decided to capture India. He was destined to play the most significant role in expanding the

Opposite: Fully decorated interior of Waz Khan mosque–Lahore.

Overleaf: A partial view of the historic Rohtas Fort built during 1542-43 A.D.

7UP
7UP

Muslim rule in this part of the world. His vigorous and systematic campaigns for the first time roused the Rajput confederacy into concerted action and a real trial of strength ensued resulting in the triumph of Muslim arms. *Muhammad Ghori* made Ghazni the base of his operations and entered upon a series of campaigns first to establish himself in the Punjab and then to push forward to the fertile valley of the Ganges.

After the death of Sultan Muhammad Ghori, *Qutb-ud-din Aibek* played an important role as he integrated the empire. Aibek fell from his horse while playing polo and died in 1210. He lies buried in a very simple tomb around Anarkali Bazar in Lahore.

After his death in 1210, he was succeeded by *Shamsuddin Altamash,* one of his former slaves. In 1211, Altamash made Delhi his capital and is regarded as the founder of the Sultanate dynasty. Delhi replaced Lahore as a seat of Muslim administration. By the beginning of the thirteenth century, therefore, the foundations of Islam in India had been laid. During the later period of the Abbasids, Persian had replaced Arabic as the vehicle of Islamic learning. Muslims in the subcontinent developed their own political, economic and religious institutions and their own centres of learning and pilgrimage. Allegiance to Islam, and the idea of belonging to a worldwide Muslim community, stimulated cultural proliferation.

Between 1206, when Qutb-ud-din Aibek succeeded to the territories of Shahab-ud-din Ghori, and 1526, there were five different dynasties with thirty-three kings. Multan was redeveloped as one of the capital cities as well as a centre of art and architecture. Even today we can see the pre-Mughal style buildings only in Multan. The tomb of *Shah Rukn-i-Alam, Shah Baha-ul-Haq* and *Shah Shamas Tabriz* are, in fact, great pieces of architecture which were built during the Tughlaq period.

The period 1200–1500 is also considered as remarkable for the spread of Muslim mysticism throughout the subcontinent.

Above left: Mughal Emperors had a passion for show of power. They were fond of fighting and wrestling. Here a Mughal Prince is enjoying the wrestling of Rams, Men, Elephants, and Camels.

Above: The Mughal miniature artists illustrated almost every aspect of life with style and perfection. Here are the three sons of Shah Jahan, Prince Shah Shuja, Prince Aurangzeb and Prince Murad.

Opposite: A side view of the Badshahi Mosque–Lahore.

Following Pages: Decorated details of Wazir Khan mosque–Lahore.

Previous Pages: Chowburji an old Mughal Monument in Lahore. In the ancient days it was the main gate of a beautiful garden.

Bab-al-Qasim, the main gate of the ancient Multan Fort.

قال عليه السلام ليس على أهل لا إله إلا الله وحشة عند الموت ولا عند القبر
قال عليه السلام من شهد أن لا إله إلا الله حرم الله عليه

The influence of Muslim mystics and their teachings are important with regard to the history of the Muslims. Islam brought in a new religion, a new civilization, new ways of thought and new values. Its rich traditions of art and literature, of culture and refinement, of social and of political institutions were established. The Sufi presentation of Islam helped to overcome religious barriers and fired the imagination of many Hindu reformers, leading to the rise of neo-Hinduism and culminating in the *Bhagti* movement which prompted several Hindu and Muslim spiritual leaders to advance the theory of the unity of all religions.

With the coming of the Mughals in 1526 A.D. a new and perhaps the most glorious epoch of Muslim rule in the subcontinent began. During the Mughal period new horizons were thrown open for the intellectual cultures. The social and political system offered opportunities of advancement and many ethnic groups accepted Islam.

Mughals are known as great builders and their architectural style is now famous throughout the world. Their building enterprise was proverbial. With generosity buildings were erected-buildings of strength and grandeur, of noble simplicity, delicacy and elegance, sometimes necessitated by their living splendour,

Above: The tomb of data Ganj Bakhsh, and the attached mosque.

Previous page: Algoza (wind pipe) musicians from Sindh. Algoza music is very popular in Pakistan.

ove: A Night view of the Shalimar
rdens–One of the Mughal monuments
Lahore.

low: A piece of glass embroidery, the most
pular craft of Baluchistan.

sometimes to mark the journey to the hereafter. Delhi, Agra and Fatehpur Sikree, the three capitals developed by them are now in India but the fourth capital which served as Dar-ul-Saltanat for many years is in Pakistan and that is Lahore. Buildings of the Mughal era are not only in Lahore but at Sheikhupura, Attock, Thatta, Peshawar and Chiniot also, which could be considered as the great pavilions of the past.

INTERESTING PLACES

THE KARAKORAMS

The most interesting areas of Pakistan are its mountain regions in the north-west. These mountains are not only the highest but the youngest mountains also and their peaks, are still rising four centimetres every 10 years.

In fact, the Karakoram and their highest peaks, deep and steep gorges, and beautiful valleys were largely unknown before 1860. The first significant attempt towards the exploration of this region was launched by *Godwin Austen* in 1861. *Austen,* at that time was serving as the Surveyor-General in the British Government of India. He surveyed the K-2 region of the Karakorams and discovered an approach to the peak, the 2nd highest peak of the world. He also crossed the Concordia–the meeting point of some of the major glaciers including Baltoro, Godwin Austen, Gasherbrum and Vinge, etc. and later he was able to reach the foot of this peak. Many Americans, British and Italian expeditions tried to conquer this peak but it defied all attempts for forty-five years. This peak was scaled for the first time by an Italian Expedition in 1954.

The mightiest Karakorams remained inaccessible thus almost invisible for centuries. Even today they are well shielded by extensive and huge mountain barriers, including the Himalayas on the south east, Hindu-Kush on the south west, the Kun Lun Chain of China on the north, the Pamirs on the west and the high, desolate plateau of Tibet on the east.

The mighty river Indus, which is one of the fifteen longest rivers of the world, forces its way through the mightiest Karakorams and the Himalayas, and snakes through Ladakh, Kashmir and the entire length of Pakistan.

The junction between the Himalayas and the Karakorams is shrouded and disguised by yet another mountain range known as Pir Panjal. These mountains are green, well forested and populated but passable only for a few summer months.

In the centre of all these mountains complex rises the Karakorams which are 400 km. (250 miles) long and over 192 km. (120 miles) wide. Protected on all sides by other mountain ranges, they form the greatest barrier on earth to the migration of people. Only its lower slopes provide a little space for scores of tribes who speak different languages.

It is now a well-known fact that the Karakorams of Pakistan are the greatest mountains on earth. In all of North America the highest peak is Mount Mckinley, Kilimanjaro 19,340 ft.; in Europe, Mont Blanc 15,781 ft., in New Zealand, Mount Cook 12,349 ft. But in the Karakorams of Pakistan, there are at least seven peaks above 26,000 ft.; K-2, 28,251 ft.; Peak 16/52 A,

)pposite: Main gate of the Badshahi
osque–Lahore.

bove: Karakorams, the highest mountains
inge of the world.

pposite: Lower Katchoora lake located
bout 20 km. from Skardu.

verleaf: The crafty people of the
ountains work hard and develop several
nall fields along the slopes for living.

26,920 ft.; Hidden Peak, 26,470 ft.; Broad Peak, 26,400 ft.; Gasherbrum-II, 26,360 ft.; Gasherbrum-III, 26,090 ft.; Gasherbrum-IV, 26,000 ft. and thirty-two others which are more than 25,000 ft. above the sea level. The great Nanga Parbat (26,660 ft.) is also one of the greatest peaks of the world though it is out of the Karakorams range.

The Karakorams confront us with phenomena that exist nowhere else on earth expect in Pakistan. Other mountain ranges are penetrable by roads and railways. But no railways cross the Karakorams and the roads are few and far between and very difficult to maintain because of frequent landslides. A appropriate proverb is very popular in the Karakoram regions and that is, "you go there of your own will but return only when allowed by the mountains". The Karakorams also serve as a watershed for the basins of the Indus and Tarim rivers. The formation of river channels for the most part, occurs in the high altitude zone; the melted waters of seasonal and perpetual snows and glaciers being principal feeders of these rivers. During winters, huge layers of ice are formed, which add to the beauty of the scenery.

The most important peak of the Himalayas in Pakistan is the Nanga Parbat 26,600 ft. It has long been regarded as the most dangerous mountain peak. There are many tales based on superstitions and many mysterious events recounted by various expeditions that failed to conquer it and also by those who finally conquered it.

Beyond the Nanga Parbat, the higher summits are all found grouped together into the Central Sector of the chain. A second chain also runs along the side of the principal chain, which after a while dips down and then gathers height again. Between the two chains there is a deep valley, almost entirely occupied by

long glaciers. It is, however, generally claimed that the deep valley of the Indus separates the chains of the Karakorams from the Western Himalayas.

In comparison to the Himalayas and the Karakorams, the Hindu-Kush is a smaller range. It covers a vast area of 400 miles long and 250 miles wide. It has several smaller peaks most of them less than 25,000 ft. high above the sea level. The highest in the range, however, is the Trichmir (25,230 ft.), called the Queen of Chitral. Trichmir along with other peaks, turns Chitral into a veritable fairy land of Pakistan. Sandwiched in these great mountains there are many valleys which allure the nature lovers from all parts of the world. Some valleys are described here for the readers interest.

BALTISTAN

Skardu is the major city of Baltistan District. It is perched at 2,438 metres (7,500 ft.) above sea level in the backdrop of the great peaks of the Karakoram mountain range.

It is linked to the national capital Islamabad by PIA which operates regular flights. Enormous rock faces rise on either side and at times it seems as if the wingtips of the plane would

Overleaf: A view of Karimabad, the major town of the Hunza Valley. High in the back-ground is the ancient Baltit fort.

Opposite: Hunza Valley – In the back-ground is the famous peak Rakaposhi.

Below: Terraced Fields–Swat.

Previous Page: Coocking flat breads in the mountain areas is an interesting process.

Opposite: The great river Indus is known for gold particals. One of the gold searchers is trying to find the gold by sheaving water and sand at the Indus Bank.

Right: One of the Pathan elders from Quetta.

Above: A view of the Kalash Dance–Bombret Valley, Chitral.

almost scrape against them. Baltistan is also known as *"Tibet-e-Khurd"* or Little Tibet since its life-style reflects that of the Roof of the World and the Land of Lamas.

Apart from its incomparable cluster of mountain peaks and glaciers, Baltistan's five valleys-Shigar, Skardu, Khaplu, Rondu and Kharmang-are noted for their luscious peaches, appricots, apples and pears. Shigar valley, 32.18 kms. (20 miles) by jeep from Skardu is the gateway to several mountain peaks of the Karakorams.

Skardu has a historic Fort atop a ridge known as the Mindoq-Khar or Castle of Queen Mindoq and three lovely lakes, that is the Upper Kachura, the Lower Kachura and Sadpara. The lower Kachura Lake 29 kms. (18 miles) and Sadpara lake 8 kms. (5 miles) from Skardu are ideal for fishing.

GILGIT

Gilgit is famous for its spectacular scenic beauty. It is only at one hour's flight from Rawalpindi. By road it takes about ten to twenty hours depending on the drivers expertise.

Lofty mountains and snow-capped peaks of the mighty Karakorams, glistening all around in the horizon, greet the visitor as he lands at the Gilgit airport. A two/three days stay here promises the visitor the pleasures and adventure of mountain climbing, mountain trekking, trout fishing or just rest pleasantly basking in the mild sun and cool fragrant mountain breeze-and some fascinating shopping.

There are many beautiful valleys within a radius of a few miles all around Gilgit. All of them are equally beautiful and inviting. These include Punial, Gupis, Phandar, Naltar, Nagar and several others. Gilgit proper serves as a spring board for all these valleys, connected by jeepable roads.

HUNZA

Hunza is surrounded by huge mountains. The terrain varies from 4,000 ft./1,219 m to 25,000 ft./7,062 m. Eternal snow, lush green orchards, murmuring streams, lovely rivers, verdant dales and emerald-green meadows are some of the charms which have made Hunza the fabled land and a "Must" for tourists.

Gilgit town is the starting point for Hunza. The valley is now quite easy to reach by air (via Gilgit) as well as by road from Islamabad. The road passes through breathtaking scenery and are generally described by travellers as "Combined heaven and earth". Apples, grapes, apricots and other fruits are found in abundance and are quite inexpensive. Karimabad, the major town of the Hunza valley, nestles at the footsteps of Rakaposhi, with River Hunza flowing below, crooning its never-ending song.

In local dialect, *Rakaposhi* means covered mountain and that is how it is always–covered with snow. There are many other peaks in the vicinity and all buried under snow.

Karimabad itself is a small town, with modest hotels and comfortable rest-houses. The entire valley, however, is famous for its peace, tranquillity, fruits, healthy water and, above all, the legend of longevity of human life. The nearby Altit offers beautiful greenery and scenery.

CHITRAL

Nestling high in the Hindu-Kush range 1,127 metres (3,700 ft.) above the sea level, the valley of Chitral is a place of fascinating scenic beauty and handsome people. Chitral's collection of rugged mountains, sulphur springs, streams teeming with trout and orchard-dotted slopes are enchanting beyond description. This valley is very popular with mountaineers, anglers, hunters, hikers, naturalists and anthropologists.

Just at an hour's flight from Peshawar, the beautiful district of Chitral is known as the land of apples, apricots, pears, pomegranates, melons and mulberries. It is a long valley about 200

Left: Village elders of Chilas.

Opposite: Foaming, gushing and rushing river Swat.

miles/ 323 kms. surrounded by Afghanistan on all sides except the south. Towards the southern-most tip of the district lie three Kalash valleys: Birir, Bomburet, and Rambur. These valleys have alpine climate. The people here are the primitive pagan tribes of Pakistan, who are known as *Kafir* or *Kalash* (wearers of black robes).

Garam Chashma is yet another beautiful valley of Chitral famous for its fruit orchards and hot sulphur springs.

The hills in the south are covered with pine *(deodar)* and fir forests. The valley is rich in mulberries, apricots, apples, pears, grapes, pomegranates and melons. There are also maple and walnut trees in the area. It offers good trout fishing.

SWAT

Swat, which is spread over 10,360 sq. kms., is the holiday makers' delight and a wonderland of magnificent scenic beauty and rich historical past. It has diversified surface upon which mountains and hilly places alternate with lowlands and planes.

Its lush green fertile valleys, towering snow-capped mountains, meandering streams, rushing torrents, ice-cold lakes, fruit-laden orchards and flower-filled slopes with smiling and dancing multicolour flowers, are some of the gifts which nature has bestowed on this ancient land.

Overleaf: Bahrain. It is one of the most popular valleys of Swat which attracts a large number of visitors every summer.

Swat has a magnificent past. It is described as *"Udayana",* (the garden), in the ancient Hindu epics; "Land of enthralling beauty", by Alexander's armies and the "Valley of the hanging chains" by Chinese pilgrims *Hieun Tasang* and *Fa-Hian*. Swat's claim to historical importance is quite as genuine as its reputation for natural beauty.

Buddhism flourished (550 B.C. – 200 A.D.) in Swat and it boasts of having more than 1,400 monasteries at one time. It is the land where great generals of the world like *Alexander, Mahmood of Ghazni, Muhammad of Ghor,* the great Mughals, *Babur* and *Akbar* fought the fiercest battles of their career. *Churchill,* who later rose to the rank of a Prime Minister of U.K., also fought here as a Lt/Captain. The picket where he spent some of the most anxious moments of his life can still be seen today.

This lovely mountain-locked region of Pakistan is now well connected with other parts of the country and the world by air as well as with an all-weather black-top motorable road. Buses and wagons leave for Swat from Peshawar and Rawalpindi–Islamabad almost every hour.

The real beauty of Swat, however, reigns in its upper valleys, Madyan 4,250 ft./1,295 M., Miandam 6,000 ft./1,818 M, Shangla 7,000 ft./2,130 M, Kalam 7,000 ft./2,130 M, Usho 8,000 ft./2,400 M, Matiltan 10,000 ft./3,000 M, Utrot 8,000 ft./2,400 M, and Gabral 8,500 ft./2,550 M. All these are extremely beautiful places and each one of them deserves two/three days stay. Comfortable rest-houses are available at all these places. Madyan, Bahrain and Kalam offer comfortable hotel accommodation throughout the year.

Swat valley changes with the seasons. In winter all the upper valleys are snow-bound; in spring (April-May) it is all riot of colours; in autumn it wears a multi-coloured floral robe. The rippling waves of River Swat rythmically makes rainbow hues in the autumn sun.

April-May are the best months to visit Swat when all its valleys are ablaze with colour. A skiing resort has also been developed in this 'vale of Valleys' at Malam Jabba about 24 miles/39 Kms. from Mingora.

DIR VALLEY

In between Swat and Chitral lies Dir, beautiful in its own rugged way. The terrain is relatively bare but mountain slopes are forested. In landscape, flora and fauna, it bears family resemblance to the sister valleys of this region.

KAGHAN VALLEY

Connected with Islamabad via three routes, Kaghan is yet another valley which offers great images. Its mountains, lakes,

Previous Page: Miandam–A beautiful Valle of Swat.

Opposite: One of the typical wooden mosques found in the mountain regions–Utrot Valley–Swat.

Overleaf: Kalam–The pride of Swat Valley.

ove: Oranges, one of the many fruits of kistan.

posite: A village elder from the Kaghan lley.

water-falls, streams and glaciers are still in an unbelievable pristine state, an unspoilt paradise.

The valley extends for 154.50 (kms. (96 miles) rising from an elevation of 2,133.60 metres (7,000 ft.) to its highest point, the Babusar Pass, at 4,145.28 metres, 13,600 ft.). Kaghan is at its best in the summer months (May to September). From the middle of July up to the end of September, the road beyond Naran, remains snow-bound throughout the winter. Movement is restricted during the monsoon season also.

One can drive in one's own or a rented car, taxi, station-wagon or bus to Abbottabad which is 115.87 kms. (72 miles) from Rawalpindi. Abbottabad is a charming town spread out over several low, refreshingly green hills.

From there it is a 72.42 kms.(45 miles) drive to Balakot, the gateway to the Kaghan valley. Balakot has the shrines of *Syed Ahmed Shaheed* and *Ismail Shaheed Brelvi, th*e subcontinent's great freedom fighters.

For going to Kaghan, one has to switch over at Balakot to a jeep. The first stop is 33.80 kms. (21 miles) away at Shogran 2,362.20 metres (7,750° ft.) above sea level. Kaghan, the little village that gives the valley its name is 61.16 kms. (38 miles) from Balakot.

At Naran, 22.53 kms. (14 miles) from Kaghan, one reaches the half-way point. Naran also serves as the base camp for the whole valley. From here one can hire a jeep or horse or hike for excursions to several picturesque lakes, valleys and peaks.

Most popular is Lake Saiful Muluk which has a touch of the unreal about it, nestling 3,200.40 metres (10,500 ft.) high under the shadows of the *Malika Parbat* (Queen of the Mountains) 5,291.33 metres (17,360 ft.) high. One can go boating on the lake and hear the local legend about *Prince Saiful Muluk* who fell in love with a fairy. Further up are quaint woodland villages, namely, Battakundi, Burawai, Besal, Gittidas and Lalazar.

The Kaghan valley, however, is blocked at the end by high mountains but a pass lets the jeepable road snake over into the Chilas valley. This is the 4,145.28 metres (13,600 ft.) high Babusar Pass, which commands the whole Kaghan panorama gives on a clear day, glimpses of the *Nanga Parbat* (Naked Mountain) glistening at 8,125.97 metres (26,660 ft.).

MURREE AND THE GALLIES

These are situated at the altitudes varying from 7,500 to 10,000 feet. The Gallies, during the summer months, are refreshingly cool, clear and crisp with plentiful of fruits and food.

Due to proximity with Rawalpindi/Islamabad/Peshawar and Abbottabad, better means of communication, and inexpensive accommodation, these valleys attract a large number of domestic as well as foreign visitors.

Murree is one such summer resort just about 30 miles/ 48 kms. from Islamabad. This hill resort attracts the largest possible number of tourists from all over the country during the summer months, i.e. May–October. During December–February Murree remains frozen under a thick quilt of snow. It wakes up from the winter slumber on week ends as tourists flock from Islamabad/Rawalpindi.

The summer brings in a great change to this region. The visitors start arriving by the first week of May and by the middle of June Murree is crowded. All hotels and restaurants are packed to capacity. From morning till late evening its roads and walks are packed with holiday crowds as are the souvenir shops and cafes.

The 'Gallies' are located in a stretch of about twenty miles on the Murree–Nathiagali–Abbottabad Road in the extreme western corner of the Hazara District. Originally the 'Gallies' were developed as a chain of hill stations where the British troops and their families were sent for respite from the unbearable heat of the plains.

About 6 miles from Murree is the small hill station known as Khaira Gali, which is 7,700 feet above sea level. Views from Khaira Gali are fascinating. The total area of this health resort is only 188 acres.

About 3 miles from Khaira Gali, on the main road, is Changla Gali, splendidly situated at an altitude of 8,400 ft. amidst thick pine forests. The 9,000 ft. Changla peak commands on one side a fine view of the Jhelum valley while on the other it presents a strikingly panoramic view of the Murree hills, the southern portion of the Hazara district and the distant plains of Rawalpindi.

Ayubia is a complex of four small hill stations namely Ghora Dhaka, Khanspur, Changla Gali and Khaira Gali. Six miles from Dunga Gali on the Murree Road is the small bazar of Kuza Gali,

pposite: Road to Ayubia, a well-known urist resort.

*ove: A view of Murree which attracts
e highest number of visitors from all
rts of Pakistan.*

from where a tarred road leads to the twin hill-resorts of Ghora Dhaka and Khanspur. At Ghora Dhaka during the summer season, a chair-lift is operated. Wild game, including bear and cheetah, is known to be found in the thickly afforested slopes.

Dunga Gali is a small resort picturesequely situated on the slopes of the Mukshpuri hill (7,800 ft.). It commands charming views of a series of wooded spurs projecting towards the river Jhelum on the western side. From Dunga Gali one can climb the 9,232 feet peak of Mukshpuri, which is the highest point in the range. Natural springs abound on the slopes.

Nathiagali, the most centrally placed and well-known of the 'Gallies' is Nathiagali. It lies midway between Murree and Abbottabad, at an attitude of 8,200 ft. and commands a fine view of the snow-capped peaks of Kashmir and Kohistan on one side and the Pothwar Plain on the other. In the foreground, to the north-east rise the green slopes of Miran Jani, about 9,000 ft. high, while in the far distance, on a clear day, may be seen the towering heights of the Nanga Parbat, with all its snow-bound majesty.

With its fascinating landscape, refreshing walks, bracing climate, beautiful ridges thickly covered with pine, chestnut, oak and maple, and above all, its quiet, calm and serene atmosphere, Nathiagali is considered to be one of the most beautiful hill resorts in the country.

HAZARA

There are many beautiful places in the Hazara District including world famous Tarbella Dam. It takes only two to three hours to reach Abbottabad, the heart of Hazara, from Islamabad by road either via Hasan Abdal or via Haripur. Abbottabad is a little town known for its educational institutions and the grand Military Academy. Abbottabad serves as a junction to go to places like Hunza, Gilgit, Baltistan, Skardu and Indus Kohistan, of the

*pposite: The Church at Nathiagali is
nely during winter.*

*verleaf: Kallar Kahar, the heart of the
an Sakesar Valley–Pothwar region.*

Karakoram Range. One can reach Swat, Swati Kohistan, Dir and Chitral of the Hindu-Kush Range. It also serves as an approach to Naran, Saiful Maluk, Shogran and Babusar Pass of the Himalayan Range. Neelum, Lipa and Jhelum valleys of beautiful Azad Kashmir and also Nathiagali or Thandyani or to Dadar etc. are reached from here.

Hazara occupies a large area, about 10,000 sq.km. and it is shaped like a tongue. To the west and north it is bounded by the Indus, to the east by Kashmir and the Jhelum river, to the south by the Murree and Margalla hills and the Rawalpindi–Attock section of the Grand Trunk Road.

Abbottabad itself is a beautiful place. It is named after *James Abbott*, Hazara's first British Deputy Commissioner. It is 1,200 metres (4,000 ft.) above sea level, and lies at the southern end of the lush plain, a wide bowl surrounded by bare brown foothills.

The Kakul Military Academy is on the hillside to the north-east of the town, the Burn-Hall boarding school lies on the Mansehra road. Cadets and soldiers can be seen marching, exercising, even practising the bagpipes.

Thandiani is a two hours drive from Abbottabad. It is situated at the northern end of the Dunga Gali range, 2,700 metres (8,800 ft) above sea level, on a small and fairly level plateau surrounded by mature pine forests.

Mansehra is only a half an hour's drive from Abbottabad. It lies in the centre of a wide fertile bowl surrounded by hills. It is very beautiful, especially in spring when everything is green against the snow-clad mountains, or in autumn when the trees change their colour.

Dadar is only a half an hour's drive from Mansehra. The road follows the boulder-strewn Siran river to Daddar, well-known for its TB Sanatorium hidden among the pine trees. It lies in a cup-shaped valley, below the snows of high hills. The hillsides are quite thickly forested, contrasting sharply with the browner tones of the Pakhili plain.

Opposite top: Bridal dresses are prepared with great care in Pakistan. Bright colour and embroidery in gold and silver are the most common features of such dresses.

Opposite bottom: Ludi, a folk dance.

POTHWAR

At the foot of the Murree hills lies the heart of Pakistan, that is, its capital Islamabad. It is located almost in the centre of Pothwar plateau which covers a large area right from Attock to Jhelum. Pothwar plateau has a diversified surface alternating between lowlands and plains, picturesque canyons and valleys. Pothwar is known as the land of flowers because the area gets maximum of rainfall in Pakistan and it is watered by the river Soan.

The physical features of Pothwar exhibit a richness and variety which, in fact, are varied in dimensions. Nature has endowed the area with some of the most beautiful scenery in

Pakistan.

During the past few years many beautiful man-made lakes have been added to the landscape of the area. There is Tarbella on the one side and Mangla on the other. In between and around the capital there are the Simly, the Khanpur, the Missriot, the Tanaza and the Rawal lakes. All of these lakes have their own charms and attractions.

Besides these gifts of nature the area occupies a unique position in the history of civilizations. The stone implements recovered from some of the terraces cut by the river Soan in the material deposited by the melting ice-fields during interglacial phases indicate that the drama of human survival was once staged here as far back as half a million years ago.

Political boundaries of this region have been varying in the different phases of history. Because of its strategic location the Pothwar mostly remained exposed to foreign adventurers and fortune seekers who criss-crossed it in their stampedes on the subcontinent like the noisy streams and rivulets of this very plateau.

Pothwar was the cradle of Buddhism which spread into Afghanistan and then to south-eastern Asia. With cities like Taxila becoming cosmopolitan centres for sociopolitical and academic activities Pothwar became the meeting ground for contemporary three religions–Hinduism, Buddhism and Zoroastrianism, until the Greeks led by *Alexander* took upon themselves to annihilate the rival Persians.

Taxila the well-known ancient site is humming with activity today as the entire area is going through an immense change–from ruins to new houses and large factories which have been set well in the lap of Margallas, as on the other side is Islamabad.

All along the Grand Trunk Road there are several places of great interest such as the Mughal Gardens at Wah, just a few kilometres from Taxila. It is believed that the gardens were laid out, on the orders of Emperor *Akbar* during later part of the 16th century. It is claimed that once Akbar stopped here and he was impressed so much by the greenery, the rivulet and the backdrop of the hills that he exclaimed, *"Wah"* which in the local language means wonderful. Keeping in view the impression of the emperor the gardens were laid out and also named as "Wah".

HASAN ABDAL

A few kilometres from these gardens the road runs through the town of Hasan Abdal. This town attracts thousands of Sikhs from all parts of the world. The famous Chinese traveller *Hieun Tsang* recorded in his memoirs that the town was sacred to the Buddhists and that there was also a tank dedicated to a serpent king, Elapatra. General *Cunningham* identified this tank with the

ht: Seeing the world for the first time: newly born parrot baby peeps out of small hole in a giant tree!

tank of the *Nag* Raja Elapatra mentioned in his accounts by Hieun Tsang.

Hasan Abdal is an interesting town with many places of great antiquity. The first is the Panja Sahib, a huge gurdawara enclosing the stone which is believed to have the impress of *Guru Nanak's* hand who was the founder of the Sikh religion. The tomb of *Baba Wali Qandhari* looks over the famous Panja Sahib of the Sikhs as well the Wah Gardens.

The third attraction is the ancient tank in which *Mahashir* fish weighing upto three to four kilo swim around undisturbed. The fourth attraction is the garden, near the tank. In the garden there is a mysterious tomb where the fabled *Lala Rukh* one of the concubines of the Emperor *Akbar* is buried. Many legends are attached with this tomb as well as with Lala Rukh, the beautiful lady who captured the heart of emperor Akbar.

TARBELLA

The Tarbella dam is located 65 km. (41 miles) from Islamabad. It is said to be the largest earth filled dam of the world. It has the largest electricity generating capacity. It also has the two biggest spillways in the world. Its water storage capacity goes into millions of tons of water. The dam is extremely impressive to visit, particularly in July and August when its lake is full of water after the monsoon rains and the melting snows. The main spillway is thrown open to carry the overflow. Sometimes both the spillways are opened to keep the stored water at a proper level. It is more than three times larger than the famous Aswan Dam on the Nile in Egypt. The 91 km. (57 miles) long lake can hold eleven million acre feet of water. The maximum depth of the lake is about 130 metres (485 ft.). The two giant spillways of the dam take an overflow of one and a half million cubic feet of water per second. It generates 3,500 megawatts of electricity. Its four tunnels at either end of the dam carry water for irrigation as well as for the electricity generation. The spillways are perhaps the most impressive feature of Tarbella for the casual visitor especially when they are thrown open between July and September. Each of the two spillways has nine enormous gates. When these are opened the overflowing water shoots down the 116 metre (350 ft.) spillways.

ATTOCK

Further up lies Attock right on the bank of the mighty Indus. Attock lives in history because of its massive fort which was built by *Akbar* the Mughal emperor for using it as defence against the invaders from Afghanistan–Akbar gave it the name of Attock Banaras in contradistinction of that of Katak Banaras, the main fort at the other extremity of his empire. A table commemorating the foundation of the fort is now over the Lahori Gate of the fort.

All around the fort there is profusion of ancient ruins, tombs, chauburjies, sarais, palaces and even pillars going right in the very bed of the mighty river Indus. Akbar used this fort, as a base camp while there was trouble at Kabul.

In 1812 *Ranjit Singh,* the Sikh ruler, seized the fort. Its occupation by Sikh troops lasted for only 10 years. The fort was later occupied by the British as a result of the first Sikh War (1846). The present buildings in the fort have been erected on the top of older ones.

PESHAWAR REGION

Beyond Attock lies Peshawar region, one of the ancient regions of Pakistan. Peshawar, the capital of the NWFP is one of the most exciting cities of Pakistan not because of its historic monuments but because of its typical atmosphere. It is very much a frontier town even today and there are major concentrations of Afghan refugees all around the city. Its many bazaars and crowded lanes give the visitor an insight into the Pathan way of life.

The origin of Peshawar seems lost in the mist of centuries, though it is mentioned in history under different names. The Chinese traveller, *Fa Hian,* who visited this part of the world in 400 A.D., mentioned Peshawar in his travelogue under the name of Po-Leusha. *Hieun Tsang,* who travelled through Peshawar in 540 A.D., recorded it as Pu-Lu-Sha-Pu-lo. Peshawar has also been mentioned by *Masudi* and *Abu Rehan* who visited this region in the 10th and 11th century as Parshawar. The city, however, retained this name till the time of *Akbar,* who Persianised it to Peshawar which is a combination of the two

Opposite: A view of one of the spill–ways of the Tarbella dam.

Persian words *"Pesh"* and *"Awar"*. The district takes its name from this principal city which is also the provincial capital of the Sarhad Province.

Till recently the city of Peshawar was enclosed with a medieval wall constructed of bricks with sixteen gates. After independence, however, there has been great expansion and new housing colonies have mushroomed all around. As such the wall has almost disappeared but some of its portions can still be seen. Most of the gates have also disappeared. These gates *(darwaza)* are (Clockwise) *Kabuli, Ander Shahar* (Asamai), *Kachehri* (Tangsali), *Reti, Rampurwa, Hashtnagari, Lahori, Ganj, Ekkatut, Kohati, Saraki, Sard Chah, Sar Asiya* (Tabiban), *Ramdas, Dabgari,* and *Bajauri.*

Set against the background of rugged hills and grey mountains, the city of Peshawar lies in the well-watered ever green valley. It is the main entrepot to the plain of Pakistan and one of the oldest cities of Asia. For over two thousand years it has been the meeting and marketing place for the people of Central Asia, the Middle East, and the subcontinent of Pakistan and India.

Lying at the mouth of the historic Khyber Pass, which links Pakistan with Afghanistan and Central Asia beyond, Peshawar, thus, became a crucible of cultures during its long span of

Opposite: Brassware on display at a shop in the Qisa Khawani Bazar, Peshawar.

Below: Mehfil-e-Milad a common religious feature.

ɔpposite top: Wild flowers as seen around ɪtchoora Lake, Skardu.

ɔpposite bottom: A Pathan elder from ·shawar.

history. Subjugated by Persians, conquered by Greeks, built by Buddhists, sacked by Seythians, destroyed by Huns, rebuilt by Brahmins, invaded by Ghaznavides, captured by Mughals, overrun by Sikhs and annexed by the British in succession, Peshawar has emerged enriched in colour and tradition from the endless turmoil of history. It still retains indelible marks of the Greeks, the Buddhists, the Persians and the Mughals. Some villages still bear Greek names and faces remind one of the classic Greek features. As the most important centre of Buddhist art and learning in the beginning of the Christian era, Peshawar and the area around it is extraordinarily rich in archaeological wealth and Gandhara sculpture.

Peshawar today is divided into three parts–the city, the cantonment and the modern residential area, including the University. The old city dates from Buddhist, Mughal and Sikh times. It is a maze of narrow streets and colourful bazaars, overlooked by the massive *Bala Hisar* Fort. The cantonment area retains the layout of the typical British Army cantonment, with its wide streets, parks, trees and imposing buildings. It is now used mainly by the Government of NWFP.

PESHAWAR ENVIRONS

The prime attractions of Peshawar, however, are the Khyber Pass, the Jamrud Fort and the Kohat Pass. Unfortunately all these places are closed for visitors.

Khyber Pass: The Khyber Pass is perhaps the most sensitive, the most historic and the most rugged of the mountain defiles which always had great strategic and economic importance. The history of the subcontinent has been greatly influenced by the success or failure of the dynasty defending it. Opening up about 11 miles west of Peshawar the Pass is guarded by the mud fort of Jamrud. Starting from the foot-hills of the *Sulaiman* Range, it gradually rises to an elevation of 3,500 feet above sea level. Two metalled roads–one above the other–have been constructed laboriously through it; the lower one for motorcars and vehicles and the upper one for camel caravans, sheep and goat herds.

Jamrud Fort: Some 11 miles from Peshawar on the Khyber road, an old battleship attracts the eye. Approaching near, it turns out to be the Jamrud Fort. Looking ruggedly majestic with its jumble of towers and loopholed walls, the fort contains the grave of its builder, the famous Sikh General *Hari Singh Nalwa,* who died here in action against the forces of the Amir of Kabul in 1837.

Kohat Pass: The tribal gun factories, whose fame has spread far and wide, lie about 25 miles south of Peshawar in a small strip of tribal territory in the Kohat Pass. Here fierce-looking tribesmen, their rosy complexions darkened by smoke, turn out hand-made weapons–pistols, revolvers, rifles and even tommy-

Above: A view of Naswari Bazaar, Peshawar.

guns. These fire-arms are exact replicas of well-known foreign makes and treasured as souvenirs by tourists.

SOAN VALLEY

The *Ghakhars* who ruled over Pothwar for sometime also built a few forts in the region. Remnants of these forts could still be seen at Rawat, Pharwala and around Lehtrar. On the Southern tip of the Pothwar stands the great Rohtas fort which was built on the orders of *Sher Shah Suri,* who ruled over India for six years–1540–45. It is, beyond any doubt, the most imposing historical monument of the Pothwar region.

The fort is about six km. in perimeter and the walls are about 30 feet thick. There are 68 towers and 12 gateways of which the most imposing is the Sohal Gate. It is a fine specimen of the Pathan style of architecture. This gate is more than eighty feet in height with exquisite balconies on the outer walls. The Sohal Gate is now used as a rest-house. The plan of the fort is adapted to suit the terrain and it is defended by a number of deep ravines as well as the river Ghaan.

About 20 kms. to the South from the fort lies the remnants of Nanda in Pind Dadan Khan sub-division. It is believed that *Al-Beruni,* the famous philosopher-scientist completed his researches here. Nearby lies the village Jalalpur which was the

ght: A shop in the (Batair Bazan Bazaar) ıail Sellers' Bazar, Peshawar.

low: The ancient way of getting otographed is still in vogue.

ove: Warsak Dam, Peshawar.

posite: A folk singer–Islamabad.

site of the historic battle (326 B.C.) fought between *Raja Porus* and *Alexander*. Raja Porus lost the battle but Alexander returned his empire keeping in view his bravery. In the west is located the greatest salt mine of the world at Khewra. Just before Khewra there are orchards of *Choha Saidan Shah* which are fed by the *Chashma Kattas*. Raj Kattas is a sacred Hindu place with numerous edifices dating from olden times with Kattas and Bhaun acquiring a prominent status in the Hindu scriptures. The Chashma, according to various legends, was caused by the wailing of *Vishnu* over the loss of his wife.

Still further west lies the beautiful hamlet of Kallar Kahar immortalized by *Babur* in his memoirs and set in scenic hills be jewelled by lovely gardens bordering an open lake and frequented by peacocks.

The world's largest salt mine is located at Khewra, a small and sleepy town about 30 kilometer from Kallar-Kahar (160 km. from Islamabad).

The existence of the salt mines has been recorded by the historians of Alexander who, it is believed, passed through the salt range on his way to battle with *Porus*. The salt range occupies several hundred square miles. The hills are low and varying in height from 2,000 to 3,250 feet above sea level. The rock formations are very interesting and in different colours varying from brown to rust and red as well as grey to green.

erleaf: Sohal Gate of the historic Rohtas rt (1542-43 A.D.).

یا اللہ مدد
786

Previous Pages: A Pothwar Landscape.

Art on wheels–One of the decorated trucks which ply on the roads of Pakistan.

A scene from Taxila Bazaar.

A close view of the Faisal Mosque, Islamabad.

Below: Murree in Spring.

ove: Flowers on display.

LAHORE REGION

From Islamabad a visit to Lahore by road is very fascinating indeed. The Highway, also called as the Grand Trunk Road, snakes through the Pothwar plateau. It is predominantly brown landscape strewn with eroded deep gullies and ravines. The scenery upto Jhelum is very interesting as there are several low hills dotted with evergreen scrubby bushes and trees as well as lowlands with small cultivated fields. Looking fresh, dazzling yellow mustard or golden or green wheat fields depending on season. However the people of the area are hardy peasants and friendly.

The first stop on the highway to Lahore is Dina about 100 km. (60 miles) from the twin-cities of Islamabad/Rawalpindi. It is one of the busiest bus stops right on the highway and offers a mixed variety of scenes. This town is developing fast because of its location. It is from here that one can also go to Rohtas Fort or to the Mangla Dam. Behind the Mangla Dam there is a beautiful lake spread over nearly 170 sq.km. with the Azad Kashmir town of Mirpur on its southern side. Overlooking the lake there is a historical fort with many legends behind it. It is believed that the fort was originally built by *Ghakhars* but much of it was altered by the Sikhs.

Jhelum is 120 km. (75 miles) from Islamabad located on the banks of the river Jhelum. It is known for its huge cantonment and the Cadets college. About 60 km. (38 miles) from Jhelum is Wazirabad.

From Wazirabad a road goes straight to Sialkot an important city located near the Indian border. There is an old fort on a hill in the town, where the representatives of the rulers took refuge during the uprising in 1857. Other places of interest are the 17th Century Tomb of *Mian Abdul Hakim,* a great Muslim scholar, and the shrine and mosque of the popular saint *Hazrat Imam*

verleaf: Faisal Mosque by Night–
ne largest mosque of Pakistan.

Above: Minar-e-Pakistan–Lahore.

Ali-ul-Haq. Allama Iqbal, Pakistan's greatest philosopher and poet, was born and raised in Sialkot. Today this town is famous for the manufacture of high quality sports goods, saddles and musical instruments.

The main highway runs through Gujranwala, which from the small town of the nineteen forties has developed into a city of repute and a major centre of trade, commerce and industry. Scores of engineering products including electrical gadgets such as fans, washing machines and cookers are produced in abundance. The area around Gujranwala also produces high quality rice.

Gujranwala was the birthplace of *Mahan Singh* and his son *Ranjit Singh* was also born here in 1780. The tomb of his father is still here. Ranjit Singh was the chief of one of the many ruling Sikh clans and eventually became master of the entire Punjab.

Lahore is nearly 65 km. (40 miles) from Gujranwala. It is one of the largest cities of south Asia and the provincial capital of the Punjab, the largest province of Pakistan. Nobody is, however, certain about the origin of Lahore. It appears that, before the Muslim invasion Lahore was an ordinary town of no importance at all. The first certain record of Lahore is that of *Hieun Tsang,* the Chinese pilgrim, who visited the city in 630 A.D. About this time it is probable that the capital of the Kingdom of

Opposite: The Shish Mahal (Palace Mirrors), a grandiose edifice inside t Lahore Fort built by Moghul Emperor Sh Jehan in 1632 A.D.

Above: Milad Chowk – Lahore.

Lahore was transferred to Sialkot, as *Alberuni* speaks of Lahore as a province with its capital at Mandhukur.

Lahore, as we know it today, reached the peak of its glory during the reign of the Mughal rulers especially during the time of Akbar who declared it his capital and held his court here for more than fourteen years from 1584–98 A.D. The later Mughal emperors beautified this city by adding scores of imperial buildings, gardens, mosques and palaces. The imperial heritage of the city is still visible as some of the works are still intact and well preserved. Lahore was captured by the Sikhs during 1770 A.D. and remained in their possession for about seventy-six years 1770–1846 A.D. The Sikhs ruled over Punjab from Lahore as well. The beauty of the Mughal monuments was destroyed as they were shorn off their decorations, marble overlays, precious and semi-precious stones and inlays by the Sikhs. This precious material was used in building the Golden temple, which is the famous religious temple of Sikhs at Amritsar (in India).

The process of destruction was, however stopped during the British period (1846–1947 A.D.) and some efforts were made to restore the beauty of Lahore by adding and constructing some of the buildings by harmoniously combining Mughal, Gothic and Victorian style of architecture. The present day High Court on the Mall, the Government College, the Lahore Museum, the National College of Arts, Lahore, the Punjab University (Old Campus), the Aitchison College and the Provincial Assembly building belong to that period.

Importance of Lahore increased manifold as the struggle for

independence was launched, in 1857. It was again at Lahore that the Indian National Congress during its mammoth meeting of 1929 resolved that India should have complete independence.

On 23rd March 1940 the All-India Muslim League in its historic session held under the chairmanship of the *Quaid-i-Azam Muhammad Ali Jinnah* unanimously adopted the Resolution on Pakistan in Lahore. So the foundation of Pakistan was laid here at Lahore.

Lahore is known for its gardens including Shalimar laid out in the reign of Shah Jahan in 1640 A.D., a great Mughal landmark. It is spread over forty-two acres with three beautiful terraces. Another Mughal garden is around *Jahangir's* tomb. Iqbal Park with *Minar-i-Pakistan* is a vast green area. The *Jinnah Garden* along the Mall offers a great variety of trees, plants, shrubs, roses and seasonal flowers. Attached to this garden is the Lahore Zoo. Many new gardens have been developed recently which offer recreational facilities as well.

Lahore is also known as the city of domes and minarets. There are hundreds of new as well as old domes and minarets. It was, primarily the Mughals who started constructing magnificent buildings majority of which were damaged during the Sikh

elow: Gulshan-e-Fatima–Lahore.

LEN 1956
vespa
vespa
LEM
1744
vespa

ɔposite top: Haran Minar, a Mughal onument built on the orders of emperor hangir.

ɔposite bottom: A bazaar view of isalabad.

ɔverleaf: Chowck Nila Gumbud, Lahore. In ɪe background is the K. E. Medical ollege.

and the British period. After independence however, the building bonanza came into full swing and continues with full speed todate. The old domes and minarets of Lahore are worth visiting. The minarets of the tomb of *Jahangir; Badshahi mosque* and *Wazir Khan's* mosque have no parallel in the country. Besides there are many mausoleums of kings, queens, princes, generals, saints and poets who created history.

Lahore, as we see it today, is different than all the Lahores of the past as described by so many historians, writers and travellers. It is no more the *Dar-ul-Saltanat* but it is the cultural, commercial, industrial, educational and political centre of Pakistan.

Lahore has more colleges than any other city of Pakistan. The Punjab University, with its Old Campus located on the Mall, just opposite the Museum and the New Campus located about ten kilometre away on both sides of the canal, is the oldest University of Pakistan.

Lahore today is the 2nd largest centre of trade, commerce, industry, employment, sports and education. So people from all parts of the province visit this city for one reason or the other.

Lahore is connected by road to various cities and towns. It takes about one hour to reach *Haran Minar* (45 km./28 miles) in Sheikhupura. It is a Mughal monument of considerable beauty and elegance. Many legends are connected with this site but the most popular is that the Minar was built on the orders of Emperor *Jahangir* in the memory of his favourite and lovely deer called *Mansraj*. Adjacent to the Minar there is a large tank and within that tank right in the centre there is a beautiful royal summer house also known as *Baradari.* It can be approached by a causeway. This building complex was in fact the recreation and hunting resort of the Mughal Emperor Jahangir. This huge tank which is 892 feet long and 570 feet wide has now been converted into a fish farm and holiday resort. Colourful looking boats are also available for rowing/peddaling.

On the outskirts of Sheikhupura is yet another important Mughal monument the Sheikhupura Fort. The tomb of *Warris Shah,* the punjabi poet laureate, is located in the village Jandiala Sher Khan nine miles from Sheikhupura. *Warris Shah* lives in the history of the Punjab as the author of *Hir–Ranjha* which is a classic work.

Another important town located near Sheikhupura is Nankana Sahib. *Guru Nanak,* the founder of the Sikh religion, was born and brought up here in this small town which is considered sacred by Sikhs.

One of the busiest highways is the Lahore–Faisalabad Road. Faisalabad which was only a small town in 1940 is the 3rd largest city of Pakistan today.

The town of Faisalabad witnessed phenomenal growth after

pposite top: A Falcon guardian in Rahim ır Khan.

pposite bottom: Wool drying in Multan.

evious Pages: A Herb Seller from ızman Mandi located at the lip or tip of eat sandy desert, Choolistan.

hildren are watching centuries old system f crushing sugarcane and extracting juice hich is used for the production of brown ugar.

independence and its population increased from 179,144 in 1951 to more than four million in 1992.

It is famous for its textile industry and fabrics manufactured in several other cities are also marketed from Faisalabad. Besides it is the largest centre of power-loom Industry in Pakistan. Beyond Faisalabad lies Sargodha, yet another important city of the Punjab.

The district derives its name for the headquarter town of Sargodha, which is a combination of "Sar" and "Godha". *"Sar"* is a hindi word which denotes a water pond while *"Godha"* was the name of the *Faqir* who lived near that pond.

The nearby town of Chiniot is famous for the fine quality furniture and the wood works. The town also boasts of its Mughal heritage. The Shahi Mosque was built during the reign of *Shah Jahan.* It is an exceedingly handsome edifice of hewn stone called *Sang-e-Larzan* obtained from various hills. The *Shah Burhan Khangah* also deserves a visit.

Jhang the nearby city of Chiniot is also famous for blankets and *khes.* The city lives in history for two romantic tales typical of the Punjab. One is the love story of *Hir-Ranjha* and another that of *Mirza-Sahiban.*

Just north of the civil station of Jhang east of the road to Chiniot, there is an ancient square tomb half-roofed with an unfinished dome which reaches little more than a foot above the spring of the arch. That is *Hir's* Tomb and the grave within is the grave of *Hir* the heroine of the famous love-story of *Hir* and *Ranjha.*

Beyond Jhang lies Thal desert spread over several thousand square kilometres. Today Thal is dotted with many villages, and towns surrounded by green fields and orchards.

MULTAN REGION

Multan is the oldest city of South Asia. It is located about 210 miles (336 km.) from Lahore and 593 miles (950 km.) from Karachi on the main Karachi–Islamabad National Highway. It is approachable by railway, road and air. There are daily flights from Islamabad, Karachi, Lahore, Faisalabad, Peshawar and D. I. Khan. This city is famous for its rich cultural heritage, important historic events, great variety of handicrafts, torid climate and profusion of legends. It is believed that *Rig Veda* was written here and the architects of Multan perfected and introduced arch in buildings and also published the first book on the art of architecture.

The recorded history of Multan goes back to the 4th century B.C. Detailed accounts of *Alexander's* invasion in 326 B.C. and his battle around Multan Fort are also well recorded. Multan also figures prominently, in the writings of the early Arab geographers. It was captured by the famous Arab General

bove: A typical household–in the
hoolistan desert.

pposite: A bazaar view of Rahim Yar
han.

verleaf: Charing Cross–the Mall–Lahore.
n the Right is the Wapda House and on
e left is the Summit Minar and the
istoric building of the Punjab Assembly
ouse.

Muhammad-bin-Qasim in 712 A.D. Multan as a state or country was ruled by Muslims for more than one thousand years though by various dynasties such as Arabs, Safwides, Samanids, Qiramties, Ghaznavid, Sultanate dynasties of Delhi, Langhas, Suris, Mughals and Pathans etc.

Being the oldest living city of the country Multan, in fact, is a story in brick and mortar telling of bygone times and people. The very walls of its Fort Complex, so often repaired and restored, the worn out steps, whisper the tales of history. The narrow lanes of the city murmer the tales of the brave people who died here while fighting for the safety of their people and their city.

Multan offers a good variety of historical monuments some of which are in good shape even today. Most of these monuments have lost their glory and many others have disappeared altogether due to ravages of time and other factors.

Even today many firsts are claimed by the Multan Division. It produces the finest and the largest quantity of Mangoes produced in Pakistan. It also produces 42% of the total wheat and more than 40% of the total cotton produced in Pakistan. It boasts of at least four monuments of the pre-Mughal period parallel of which cannot be seen in any other part of Pakistan; that is, the tomb of *Shah Rukn-i-Alam* the tomb of *Baha-ud-Din Zakaria* the tomb of *Shah Shams Sabazwari* and the tomb of *Yusaf Shah Gardez.* Some of the handicrafts produced in Multan are also of unique type and sold in almost every major city of the country.

While around Multan do not forget to visit Bahawalpur which is a city of recent origin. It was developed in 1780 A.D. on an old site.

Today's Bahawalpur is famous for its Islamic University, Tabia College and the largest National Park known as *Lal Sohanra.*

7UP

The palaces of the ex-rulers are mainly located in *Dera Nawab Sahib* about 35 km. from Bahawalpur except the *Daulat Khana* palace.

LAL SUHANRA NATIONAL PARK

The park is ideal for recreation, education or research and shooting is forbidden. The park, 22 miles (36 km.) to the east of Bahawalpur, is a combination of natural lake, forest and desert spread over 77,480 acres of sandy land on both sides of the Bahawal canal. There are many watch towers, tourist huts, rest-houses, camping grounds and treks for the visitors.

Choolistan the famous desert is 30 km. from Bahawalpur and *Yazman Mandi* may be considered as the starting point. The desert is spread over an area of 16,000 sq.km. overlapping into the Indian desert of Rajasthan. The whole area was once well watered by the River Ghaggar, known by various names in the past such as Sarsavati, Sutudari, Wahindat and now called as Hakra. All along the 312 miles (500 km.) of the dried up river there are more than 400 archaeological sites. It is believed that these sites, if excavated will provide the missing links between Moenjodaro and Harappa the two principal sites of the Indus Valley. Choolistan also has many old forts such as Derawar, Vingrot, Banwar, Marcot, Wilhar, Maujgarh Mao, Phulra and Dingarh, etc.

Derawar is still in a good condition. Its rampart walls are intact and it is guarded even today by the personal guards of the ex-Amir of Bahawalpur. The tombs of the ex-rulers of Bahawalpur and their families are located in this fort. The tombs have glazed blue tile work, prior permission, however, is necessary from the Amir of Bahawalpur for entering the fort.

The most important feature of Choolistan is sand and its formations. These dunes, although in theory are for practical purposes fixed, permanent landmarks in the sea of shifting sand. In places vast accumulations of sand weighing millions of tons move inexorably in regular formations, growing, retaining their shape, is vaguely disturbing to an imaginative mind.

Another important feature of Choolistan is its wildlife. This desert boasts of Nilgai, Chinkara deer, Hog deer, Black buck, Fox, Jackal, Hare, and Wild Cats, Larks, Owls, Baz, Bashin, Tamtari, Crows, Parrots, and Sand Grouse are also found in abundance. Besides there are various species of lizards, and rats, etc.

From Bahawalpur or from Multan it takes about three hours to visit Uchh, a town of great antiquity. This town has been associated by some historians with one of the many Alexandrians built by *Alexander* on his way down the Indus in 326 B.C. *Arrian* the military historian writing in the 2nd century A.D. records that "Alexander ordered a city to be built on the confluence of the two rivers, imagining that by the advantage of such a situation it would become rich and prosperous."

No doubt Uchh is located at the confluence of the river Sutlej and the Chenab but it is difficult to understand as to why an invader would build a city while on his way and facing many difficulties. Nevertheless Uchh is there and lives in history as one of the ancient centres of learning and architecture. It is also famous for its beautiful shrines ornamented with blue mosaic and other embellishments executed in stuco and other materials. Its great period of glory came in the thirteenth century, when it became, together with Multan, a great centre of political, cultural and literary activities. This independent kingdom attracted many eminent poets, writers, religious scholars and saints from various parts of central Asia. The kingdom, no doubt, lasted for only a short period but the city continued to attract religious scholars and saints even after its political downfall. It is believed that more than two and a half thousand scholars worked in the great institution of Islamic learning which was established by *Hazrat Saifuddin Gazaroni,* a person of great learning and knowledge, who came here from Baghdad in 993 A.D.

Hazrat Jalal-ud-Din Bokhari Surkhposh (saint in the red robes) whose tomb, attracts a large number of people from all parts of Pakistan even today, is also known for his great learning and services for the promotion of Islamic learning and literature. He had also migrated from Bokhara and settled here.

The tombs of Uchh are built on the pattern of the Multan tombs with certain local architectural additions. The tomb of *Bibi Jawindi* which appears to be complete from one side, is octagonal in shape. Most of the Uchh tombs are now falling apart as

elow: A desert scene from Choolistan.

they are not being looked after well.

The Panjnad head works is only 9.4 miles (15 km.) from Uchh. Panjnad is known for its grand irrigation system as well as the fact that the famous five rivers of the Punjab merge into the great Indus at Mithankot just a few kilometre away. The Panjnad headworks may even be considered as the only bridge which separates as well as connects the two deserts, that is Choolistan and Thal. In fact the highway from Multan to Karachi via Muzaffarghar–Alipur etc. goes through Thal and crosses the great river system at Panjnad.

Mithankot has become a place of reverence for containing tombs of a number of saints. Of these most famous is the shrine of *Khawaja Ghulam Farid* a well-known Sufi Poet of *Saraiki* language. His Kafies are known far and wide for the sweetness and pathos. The saints of Mithankot were spiritual guides of the rulers of Bahawalpur and leading families of Rahimyar Khan, Multan, Muzaffargarh, and Dera Ghazi Khan districts.

Choolistan in fact overlaps the Thar desert of Sindh which overlaps the Indian desert of Rajasthan. However the people who live in these three deserts are different ethnically as well as culturally. But Choolistan is changing very fast indeed. The roads and canals net works have changed the entire life style of the Choolistan people. The long lines of camels, which were the only sure system of communication and transportation till few years ago, have been replaced by tractors and trollies.

SINDH

Rohri is an important town, a busy railway station and a junction of the Pakistan Railways on the main Karachi-Peshawar line. From here a branch line takes off to Sibi–Quetta–Chaman after crossing the river Indus over the Ayub bridge. The interest in the town mainly lies in its antiquities. There is a mosque of moderate appearance said to have been built in about 1545 A.D. for the reception of the *'Moo-e-Mubarak'*–a hair of the beard of the *Holy Prophet* (pbuh). The hair encased in a box is exhibited annually on the nineth day of Zilhaj, but it is shown to visitors at all times. Another important building of interest is the Jamia Masjid built about 1583 by one *Fateh Khan* an officer in the army of the Emperor *Akbar*. There is a hill of seven virgins which consists of a row of small rooms connected by a long passage cut partly of rock and ornamented externally with coloured tiles. It is believed that seven virgin sisters are buried here. Many legends have been spun around these graves which are wrought with decorations, and stone carvings. The graves are similar in shape and size as those seen at the Chowkundi tombs. Opposite to the city of Rohri there is a small island which contains the shrine of the *Zinda Pir Khwaja Khizar* and it is visited both by

Opposite: A mosque near Sukkhur, Sindh

ght: A Bazaar view from Umar Kot, Thar
esert–Sindh.

pposite: A Crane catcher of Larkana, Sindh.

Muslims and Hindus alike.

The nearby town of Alrore or Arore, which lies about five miles to the south-east of Rohri, is a place of considerable historical importance. It is believed to be the ancient capital of Sindh and a place of residence of King *Dahir* at the time of the conquest of Sindh by the Arabs under *Muhammad-bin-Qasim* in 711 A.D.

The town of Sukhur is situated on the right bank of the river Indus; on the opposite bank of the river is the town of Rohri and about midway in the stream between Sukhur and Rohri is the Bakhar island (a fortress) and a little southward and nearer to the Sukhur town is the wooded island of Sadhu Bella. It is decorated with very unusual type of tile work having no traditional pattern and profusely carved marble tiles.

The new Sukhur is well built and is generally clean and tidy besides being well drained. It is comparatively of modern origin and owes its existence to the location of British troops stationed in 1839 at the time when Bakhar Fort was made over to the British by a treaty by the *Mirs* of Khairpur.

The most prominent feature of the Old Sukhur is the tomb of *Khair-ud-Din* which was built in 1758 A.D. The other antiquities of Sukhur are the Tomb of *Adam Shah* and the Minaret of *Masum Shah.* The latter, and the most conspicuous structure was built in about Hijri 1027 (1607 A.D.), by *Mir Muhammad Masum,* a famous Syed soldier whom Emperor *Akbar* appointed as Nawab of Sukhur. Sukhur is also famous for bridges: The Lansdowne bridge connects Rohri with Sukhur and is a place of great interest for tourists. It was the first cantilever (suspension) bridge, built over Indus 70 years ago the total span being 790 feet and it was considered a great engineering feat.

The Ayub Bridge has been named after the ex-President of Pakistan, Field-Marshal *Muhammad Ayub Khan.* This bridge was designed by *Dr. D. D. Steinman* of New York. It is the third longest railway arch bridge in the world, after the Sidney

verleaf: Women of Thar have to work hard
nd travel long distances just to get some
otable water.

Harbour Bridge of Australia and the Hell Gate Bridge of the U.S.A.

The Sukhur Barrage is also worth seeing. As many as seven canals rush out of this Barrage which irrigate thousands of acres of land in Sindh and some parts of Baluchistan. In fact fertility of the entire province of Sindh depends on these large water works.

KOT DIJI

About 20 miles from Sukhur, on the national highway, surrounded by date-palm orchards is Kot Diji. The people who lived here were the forerunners of the Indus Valley Civilization. During the Muslim period it was, known as Ahmadabad. In the 18th Century, *Mir Fateh Ali Khan Talpur,* who was the then Ruler of Sindh, shifted his capital from Khudabad (near Sehwan) to Hyderabad and divided his kingdom into seven parts. To the west of Diji, a fort is situated on the hill. Approach to the fort is through three strong gateways on the east, each situated on a different terrace. The fort which runs north-south in a narrow strip has no significant residential building, except a house to the right of the entrance gate and narrow chambers running along the defences. A pavilion built in a beautiful cut-stone work commands the eastern defence and was probably the seat of the Nawab during the peace times.

From Sukhur it takes only four to five hours to reach Moenjodaro, once capital city of the Indus valley civilization. The road is good and passes through green paddy field and small villages. The locals are very fond of music. The common musical instruments used are flute and *Algoza.* Dancing is not prevalent here.

At the time of the invasion of Sindh by *Muhammad-bin-Qasim*

Opposite: Decorated pony waiting for the riders–Karachi Beach.

Below: A Camel Caravan–Thar Desert–Sindh.

in 712 A.D. the famous Hyderabad fort was in the possession of the Buddhists. It was surrendered to the young Arab General on his arrival after the fall of Debal. In the 16th and 17th centuries it continued only as the district headquarters under the Arghun rule who had capital of Sindh at Thatta.

In 1757 the Indus changed its course resulting in over-flooding the old capital of the Kalhoras, in district Dadu. *Ghulam Shah Kalhora,* the then ruler of the territory changed the name of the town from Nirankot to Hyderabad, after the name of *Hazrat Ali* (known also as Hyder).

In 1783 A.D. Kalhora dynasty was overthrown by the Talpurs and the conqueror *Mir Fateh Ali Khan* shifted to Hyderabad and rebuilt the entire town.

BHIT SHAH

35 miles from Hyderabad, is the famous resting place of *Shah Abdul Latif Bhitai* (1689–1772 A.D.), the great poet saint of Sindh. Bhit Shah is situated to the north-east of Hyderabad and about two miles to the east of the National Highway in the Hala Taluka of Hyderabad District. Hala itself is now a district. Bhit Shah is a small village spread over four square miles, with a population of 3,000 people. Shah Abdul Latif, whose poetry, thought and philosophy is a beacon to all mankind, chose this *"Bhit"* (sand dune or mound) as his permanent abode in 1744. Over his grave, *Ghulam Shah Kalhora,* first of the Kalhora rulers, raised, a beautiful mausoleum in 1758 A.D. Later *Mir Naseer Khan Talpur, Mir Nur Muhammad Khan Talpur* and *Mir Muhammad Khan Talpur* contributed to the beautification of the shrine and the mosque.

HALA (OLD AND NEW)

Old Hala is an important town situated in the north of the district on the bank of Indus, two miles from new Hala. New Hala is the resting place of *Makhdoom Nooh,* a great saint of Sindh. It is situated on the National Highway about 40 miles (64 km.) from Hyderabad. The place is famous for its handicraft industry. Tiles, handloom manufacture of *"sousi"* and *"ajrak"* cloth, and embroidery work. A cattle fair is held in Hala on the first Monday of every lunar month.

HYDERABAD

Though a very old and historical city yet Hyderabad does not boast of grand palaces or forts. There is only one fort which lies in ruins. The only monument of historical interest in Hyderabad, are the tombs of the *Mirs.* They lie on the northern extreme of the ridge on which the town of Hyderabad is built.

After independence, some new townships have been set up such as Shah Latifabad Colony to the south, the Industrial Trading Estate to the east, Liaquat Medical College and Jamshoro are towards the north-west of the city. The creation of these new townships has considerably expanded the area of the city and enhanced the beauty of Hyderabad.

RANIKOT FORT

About 56 miles (90 km.) north of Hyderabad, there is a small town *"Sann"*. From here a track for 13 miles (21 km.) leads to Ranikot Fort through uninhabited country. The most magnificent portion of the Ranikot Fort is Shahper gate which offers the longest, unbroken resemblance of the 'Great Wall' of China. It is claimed to be one of the largest forts in two world. Nobody knows for sure about the builders of this fort. It stands there lonely and mysteriously on the Kirthar Mountains, its origins unknown.

AMRI

It is about 12 miles (20 km.) north of *"Sann"*. More than 20 acres of ancient mounds have been partially excavated here. It is believed that the inhabitants predated the Indus valley civilization. These people, however, disappeared mysteriously when the Indus people rose to power around 2500 B.C.

SEHWAN SHARIF

Next is the town of Sehwan Sharif which is one of the oldest

low: Twilight along the Indus–Sehwan.

Left: Mosque Eidghah, Hyderabad–Sindh.

Overleaf: Karachi by Night–Zaib-un-Nisa Street.

RAMZAN & SON
TAILORS
ALICO
ALICO LTD
BISCUITS

IGNIS
UNICARD

towns of Sindh. It rises on the top of a conical hill, and nearby lies the ruins of a huge fort believed to have been founded by *Alexander.*

Sehwan was the capital of a Buddhist ruler who was the brother of *Chandragupta II,* the third of the Gupta dynasty in the fourth century A.D. From the time of the Arab invasion in 711 A.D. Sehwan figures constantly in the history of Sindh, as it commanded the route from the upper to the lower Indus, through which all invaders from north had to pass. So possession of the fort was essential for the success of every campaign.

Sehwan is now famous for the shrine of *Lal Shahbaz Qalander,* a saint whose real name was Sheikh Usman Ali. *He* came from Marand in Persia and belonged to the *Qalanderiyah* order of dervishes. Born in 1177 A.D. he was not only a sufi and a missionary, but a scholar, a poet and a philologist who wrote several books in Persian and Arabic.

MANCHAR LAKE

A few miles to the west of Sehwan Sharif lies the largest lake of Sindh known as the Manchar Lake. During the rainy days this lake spreads over 500 to 1,000 square kilometres. The lake abounds in several kinds of fish and birds. A large colony of fishermen, the *Mirbars,* live here on large wooden boats.

KARACHI

"One day she will be the Queen of the East", said *Charles Napie*r a hundred years ago about Karachi. It was then only a small village. Today Karachi bursts upon the visitor as a vast commercial and industrial centre, a sea of people teeming with human activity, its population having already exceeded nine million mark and still growing.

This metropolitan city of Karachi was until 1725 A.D. just a barren piece of land, washed on three sides by the blue waters of the Arabian Sea. A few fishermen lived in small huts on the sunny creek. There was a pool of water on this barren piece of land which was known as Kalachi-jo-Kun. *'Kalachi'* was the name of a fisherman whereas *'Kun'* meant a deep ditch. Therefore, *"Kalachi-jo-Kun"* meant the deep ditch of Kalachi, the fisherman.

A few mud huts sprang around this point and their numbers increased. Gradually a village came into being. This village was called as *Kalachi-jo-Ghote,* which as time passed grew into prominance.

By 1900 Karachi established itself as one of the important wheat exporting ports of the east. Karachi also played an important role during the First World War (1914-18), for the allied forces. Being on the direct sea route, Karachi-Basra link became the main supply route for food and equipment.

Opposite: A view of the Karachi port. In the foreground is the towering office of the National Shipping Corporation.

The Second World War (1939-45) further boosted its development considerably.

The city is less than three hundred years old. From the small fishing village it was turned into a military cantonment and then developed as a small seaport. This port sprang into prominance and became the capital of Sindh. When Pakistan came into being – Karachi became the capital of Pakistan as well as the chief port of the country.

Thousands of people flocked into Karachi from all parts of the subcontinent. So its population swelled. The new comers brought money, labour, technology and management with the new government providing unprecedented facilities to the business community a new class of merchants came into being–and Karachi became not only the largest city of Pakistan but also the largest industrial and commercial centre of Pakistan within a few years after the Independence.

erleaf: A view of Karachi City.

pposite: The tomb of Quaid-e-Azam ıhammad Ali Jinnah, Karachi.

low: Paradise Point–Karachi.

Above: The Presidency–Ziarat, Baluchistan.

Opposite: A carpet seller at the main bazaar, Quetta.

BALUCHISTAN

Quetta is the capital of Baluchistan which is the largest province of Pakistan area-wise. It is surrounded on all sides by the barren mountains that burn in the summer and freeze in the winter. The town derives its name from two localities, that is, Quetta and Peshin. *Kwatta* which is now spelt as Quetta, means a fort within the walls of which the old town was situated. Pishin is a modernised form of *Pushang* which is old Persian for the Arabic Pushaj.

The Quetta as we see today is much different than the old Quetta which was destroyed on May 31, 1935 by an earthquake. More than 30,000 persons lost their lives, and property worth hundreds of millions of rupees was completely perished. The city generally looks like a frontier town. It is surrounded by mountains intersected by long, narrow valleys. The mountains are fairly uniform in character consisting of long central ridges.

Much of the Baluchistan is a high barren plateau 1,000 to 1,250 metres (3,000 to 4,000 ft.) above sea level, enclosed by the Toba Kakar mountain range along the Afghan border and by the Sulaiman Range which borders the Indus river. To the south lies one of the most inhospitable deserts in the world, the Makran, which nearly defeated Alexander when he marched through it on his way home. It is wild, rugged, and sparcely populated country bordering Afghanistan and Iran. The formidable mountain ranges and the character of the Baluchi people make Baluchistan an imposing and dramatic area to visit.

Very little is known of the history of Baluchistan upto the thirteenth century. It is, however, certain that the area formed part of the kingdom of Amir Subaktagin and Mahmud Ghaznavi, and passed to their successors, the *Ghori* dynasty of Ghazni.

Opposite top: Jinnah Avenue–Quetta.

Opposite bottom: A Stone Breaker working on the Quetta–Sibi Road, Baluchistan.

Overleaf: One of the grand mosques of Quetta, Baluchistan.

Towards the end of the 14th century it was captured by *Timur* and conferred by him to his grandson *Pir Muhammad.*

In the 16th century a great warrior, *Ameer Chakar Rind,* united the main Baluchi tribes with the force of good words and sword. The British first came to Baluchistan during the First Afghan War in 1839–42. Although the *Khan* was killed in 1840, the British returned occupied lands to his sons after withdrawing from Afghanistan. In 1854 they stationed a political agent there.

After the annexation of the Punjab, the British pursued their forward policy of strengthening the borders of British India against possible Russian invasion. By 1887, all of Baluchistan was in British hands, and in 1993 the *Durand Line,* the border between British India and Afghanistan, was fixed.

Some Baluchi authors claim the origin of their people to the biblical *Nimrod* 4,500 years ago, or to the Syrian god *Baal,* or to *Balu* and his followers the *'Baluchis'.*

Most of the people of Baluchistan live around Quetta within a radius of about eighty miles (130 km.). The city does not have any historical or archaeological places of any importance. Some mounds, however, have been recently discovered close to the city dating back to Moenjodaro period (2500 B.C.)

Quetta district is rich in scenic beauty. The Hanna and Urk valleys are worth seeing particularly during the summer when the apple orchards are in full bloom. These valleys produce the finest Kulu apples. The nearby *Hanna* Lake and the water reservoir of *Spinkerez* are also populartourist resorts.

Mr. Barnes the first "Political Agent" or Administrator of Quetta has described Quetta in the following memorable words:

> "Quetta and Pishin have beauties of their own which vary with each season of the year. In the spring, after rains, the whole countryside, even on the slopes of the hills are tinged with green and everywhere the ground is studded with wild flowers. Red and yellow tulips, similar to those found in the fields of Florence, nestle in the depressions of the lower hills, wild hyacinth and irises of various hues abound among the rocks and stones, the ground in many places is scarlet with the small red poppy, and all around the air is fragrant with faint aromatic odour of the fresh southern wood which covers the uncultivated plains.
>
> Summer is less gorgeous; but, the harvest is cut in June, the country around Quetta itself is a sheet of waving corn-fields. July, August and September are hot, dry, dusty and depressing, but early in October frost appears at night, the dust clears out of the sky, and the perpetual sunshine, the dry, keen invigorating air, the clear atmosphere and glorious rose-coloured tints of the hills at sunset and sunrise are a constant joy to a lover of the beautiful scenes.
>
> In winter, the scene changes again and though the country is

Above: Mosque, Yek Minara–Quetta.

Opposite: Jamia Mosque, Ziarat, Baluchistan.

arid and drab-coloured, and the leaves are off the trees, still few places are more beautiful than Quetta on a bright, still, frosty morning, when all the lofty peaks round the valley are capped with glistening snow".

The entrance into Quetta district is through the historic *Bolan Pass.* The Pass is about fifteen miles and commences from Machh. The railway line threads its circuitous route through many tunnels and bends and emerges into the Quetta Plain at Kilpur. The drive through the narrow Bolan Pass is, in the opinion of many visitors, spectacular. The best months to go through it are April and October when the large camel caravans of the nomads are on the move to and from the summer pastures on the higher ground. In olden times it was the main route to the subcontinent from Central Asia, and has remained the chief route to the subcontinent from Kandahar and Herat in Afghanistan. The British also passed through it from India on their way to fight the First Afghan War.

The Bolan Pass in fact is the valley of the Bolan river. It consists for the most part of rugged and barren hills dotted here and there with green fields along the bank of the river and clusters of houses. The traveller's eye is attracted to the black spots cut into the hillside. These are the openings to the sharts of coalmines. However, the most picturesque of the Passes in Quetta district is the Khojak Pass which connects Quetta with Chaman on the other side of the Khojak Range. Through it passes the Khojak rail tunnel which is one of the longest railway tunnels in the world. The highest point is the Khojak Top which is 7,700 feet above sea level.

Bolan Pass, is the most important Pass through which Quetta is connected with the hinterland. Just a few kilo-metre beyond Bolan Pass (on the Sibi side) around eight kilometre from the

لا اله الا الله محمد رسول الله

main highway, Mehar Ghar is located.

Just before Sibi the view opens up as the hills of the Brahui Range become visible in the distance. The road to the Bolan Pass bypasses the town, but it is worth making a detour into the centre, if only to see the Chakar's old mud fort, which is clearly visible from the railway crossing. The town of Sibi is quite old, and its setting attractive. The town boasts one of the highest summer temperatures ever recorded in the subcontinent. In February tribesmen from all over Baluchistan flock to Sibi to attend the colourful Horse and Cattle fair.

In the early 16th century *Ameer Chakar Rind,* who united the Baluchi tribes, defeated here the ruler of the Sammah dynasty. His fort can still be visited near the town. The British briefly occupied Sibi in 1841, on their way to the First Afghan War, but it was not until 1879 that it was officially handed back to them. *Sir Robert Sandeman* negotiated with the *Marri* and *Bugti* tribesmen here during his pacification of the area.

Below: Lotus lake–Islamabad.